BARE BONES YOUNG ADULT SERVICES

Tips
for Public
Library
Generalists

Renée J. Vaillancourt

Public Library Association

Young Adult Library Services Association

AMERICAN LIBRARY ASSOCIATION
Chicago and London   2000

While extensive effort has gone into ensuring the reliability of information appearing in this book, the publisher makes no warranty, express or implied, on the accuracy or reliability of the information, and does not assume and hereby disclaims any liability to any person for any loss or damage caused by errors or omissions in this publication.

The section "Reference and Homework Support" in chapter 6 was written by James Rosinia and published in 1993 by the Public Library Association and the Young Adult Library Services Association in the book *Bare Bones: Young Adult Services Tips for Public Library Generalists*.

Text design by Dianne M. Rooney

Composition by the dotted i in New Aster and Univers using QuarkXPress 3.32 for a Macintosh

Printed on 50-pound white offset, a pH-neutral stock, and bound in 10-point coated cover stock by Documation

The paper used in this publication meets the minimum requirements of American National Standard for Information Sciences—Permanence of Paper for Printed Library Materials, ANSI Z39.48-1992. ∞

Library of Congress Cataloging-in-Publication Data

Vaillancourt, Renée J.
    Bare bones young adult services : tips for public library generalists / by Renée J. Vaillancourt. Public Library Association [and] Young Adult Library Services Association.
        p.   cm.
    Includes bibliographical references and index.
    ISBN 0-8389-3497-8
    1. Public libraries—Services to teenagers—United States.
I. Public Library Association.   II. Young Adult Library Services Association.   III. Title.
    Z718.5.V35   2000
    027.62'6—dc21   99-35643

Printed in the United States of America.

04   03   02   01   5   4   3   2

CONTENTS

FIGURES

ACKNOWLEDGMENTS

One of the greatest things about working in the field of librarianship is the generosity and support of professional colleagues. *Bare Bones Young Adult Services* is truly a collaborative effort—dozens of librarians, educators, and writers generously contributed training materials, allowed me to reprint their publications, and shared their knowledge and experiences in response to my electronic discussion list postings or direct queries about topics covered in this book.

I would like to thank the following people in particular, without whom this book would not have been possible:

Patrick Jones, Jane Byczek, Andrea Glick, and Cathi Dunn MacRae for encouraging me to write about young adult librarianship and for helping me figure out what I had to say;

Mary K. Chelton, one of the editors of the early version *Bare Bones: Young Adult Services Tips for Public Library Generalists* (1993), for recommending that I write another and for providing her help and support along the way;

All of the "Serving the Underserved" trainers and other contributors (especially Patrick Jones, Judy Druse, Dana Burton, and Jane Byczek), who were so generous in granting permission to reprint their work;

Linda Waddle of YALSA and Kathleen Hughes of PLA for their editorial support and unwavering enthusiasm;

Pam Barry, who inspired my ideals of youth participation and who set the standard of library service that I aspire to;

The members of the Teen Advisory Board in Lincoln, Rhode Island, and the Teen Library Council in Carmel, Indiana, who turned me on to young adult services;

My parents, Mary and Raymond Vaillancourt, who, by encouraging me to read widely as a teen, were my first role models as advocates of intellectual freedom;

And my husband, Sean McGrath, who sacrificed too many weekends to this book and who chopped more wood than we could ever burn in one Montana winter so that the house would be quiet and warm for me to work in.

Mary K. Chelton and James M. Rosinia co-authored the predecessor to *Bare Bones Young Adult Services*. Entitled *Bare Bones: Young Adult Services Tips for Public Library Generalists*, it was published jointly by the Public Library Association and the Young Adult Library Services Association in 1993. Rosinia was the sole author of "Reference and Homework Support" that appears in both titles.

INTRODUCTION

The poet Gabriela Mistral wrote, "Many things we need can wait, children cannot. Now is the time when their bones are being formed, their blood is being made, their minds are being developed. To them we cannot say tomorrow; their name is today." Young adults, as well as children, cannot wait for libraries to provide services; their future is today and now is the time to shape that future.[1]

In 1994, the first national survey of young adult services in United States public libraries, *Services and Resources for Children and Young Adults in Public Libraries,* found that, although 23 percent of all library patrons are young adults between the ages of twelve and eighteen, only 11 percent of all public libraries have a young adult specialist on staff.[2] In some libraries, teens are served by children's or youth services librarians. In others, young adult services are the responsibility of the reference department. And many libraries still fail to provide any specific services for young adults at all.

As the generation of twelve-to-eighteen-year-olds continues to increase across the country, we can no longer afford to neglect this substantial segment of the population. The primary audience for *Bare Bones Young Adult Services* is the library generalist—a staff member who provides services to teens as well as to other segments of the population. If you are a librarian responsible for young adult services in addition to your traditional area of expertise, a media specialist making the transition from an elementary to a secondary school, or a new young adult specialist without any formal training in librarianship, this manual will serve as an excellent starting point in learning how to provide quality library service to teens.

Since an early version, *Bare Bones: Young Adult Services Tips for Public Library Generalists*, was published, the Internet has become a dynamic forum for communication about library services. Electronic discussion lists such as PUBYAC and YALSA-BK host lively discussions about young adult services and literature, and Web sites hosted by the American Library Association (ALA) and other organizations provide invaluable information about ways to serve teens in libraries.

The Young Adult Library Services Association (YALSA), a division of ALA, has also trained a corps of young adult specialists to teach other librarians how to improve service to teens. These "Serving the Underserved" (SUS) trainers have conducted hundreds of workshops all over the country and have found themselves in great demand by librarians who are eager to learn more about ways to meet the needs of young adults.

Bare Bones Young Adult Services addresses many of the frequently asked questions (FAQs) raised on the electronic discussion lists and in the SUS training workshops. It includes practical information about ways to involve teens in planning for library service to young adults and ideas for successful young adult programs. It also addresses questions about ways to make effective use of technology and the Internet with teens in the library and how to establish a successful young adult area and collection.

Bare Bones Young Adult Services is a hands-on guide to the philosophy and practice of young adult services. It is intended to provide practical ideas on how best to meet the needs of teenagers in the library.

In an age in which there is a politically correct term for nearly every subsection of the American population, people between the ages of twelve and eighteen have been sadly overlooked. Most teens I know refer to themselves as "kids." Librarians tend to use the term "young adult." In this manual, this target population is referred to as teenagers, teens, young adults, or "YAs" for short, with all due respect to the "kids" themselves.

NOTES

1. Jane Byczek, Youth and Young Adult Services, Hinsdale, Ill., Public Library.
2. U.S. Department of Education, Office of Educational Research and Improvement, National Center for Education Statistics, *Services and Resources for Children and Young Adults in Public Libraries* (Washington, D.C., U.S. Government Printing Office, 1995).

Young Adult Services Philosophy

Why Serve Teens?

For an audience struggling through the introduction of free will—taking on the curse of responsibility while still subject to the often impenetrable logic of parental guidance—the lesson of banal, quotidian injustice and necessary falsehoods is both heartbreaking and essential. And being reminded that maturity means loosening your grip on clear distinctions between right and wrong as well as tightening your hold on your own emotions is at once more pertinent and universal than an adult reader might expect.[1]

With the recent increase in the severity and number of incidents of violence in schools and other public places, parents, teachers, and librarians are left wondering what they can do to help troubled youth. Recent studies have shown that teens feel less equipped to deal with emotions like anger, frustration, and loneliness than with other problems that they encounter. "Twenty-five percent [of teens say that] not having an adult to talk to about problems and decisions is a serious concern for themselves and their friends. . . . Those areas in which young people feel they have received sufficient adult guidance are

1

also generally the areas in which they feel most sure that they have made the right decisions."[2] Public librarians, who influence teens outside of the mandated realms of home and school, are in an ideal position to fill that role.

According to a 1994 Department of Education report, public high school enrollment is expected to increase 13 percent between 1997 and 2007.[3] Even if the numbers alone don't warrant providing special library service to young adults, consider that all these teenagers will soon be tax-paying adults who will vote for or against library funding in many communities.

Perhaps more importantly, teenagers are citizens experiencing a significant transition in their lives. For many people, adolescence is the first time they begin to think about the "big issues" that will affect their future. They begin to question their parents and other authority figures who have taught them what to believe and how to behave. They start to form opinions for themselves. For this reason, libraries need to provide unbiased information on a wide variety of topics so that young adults can gather the knowledge they so desperately need to develop and grow.

I was spending the afternoon in the usual place—my local library, doing whatever it was I liked to do then, when suddenly . . .

She entered my life.

She was a woman who would change my destiny.

She was a woman who would later ask me to condense my entire life on one short page of a foreword.

She introduced me to a youth participation group she had recently started at the public library.[4]

Teens are often interested in controversial topics. Subjects such as sexuality, religion, drug and alcohol use, music, philosophy, and psychology are often explored for the first time during adolescence. Reading and talking about these issues allow teens to discover how they feel about things, which leads to an understanding of who they are on a variety of levels. It is essential to their healthy development.

Some of the greatest incentives for serving teens in libraries are the personal benefits gained by all. Young adults who are included in the planning process in libraries develop a sense of camaraderie and improved self-esteem. Librarians who work closely with teens have the satisfaction of stimulating library use while improving their ability to serve this segment of the population. For many young adult specialists and for generalists who serve them, seeing teenagers excited about reading and using library materials, and serving as a mentor to young people, are some of the most rewarding aspects of their profession.

Teachers use the slogan "I touch the future—I teach." Librarians also carry the great responsibility of affecting the life of a growing person. Patrick Jones, author of *Connecting Young Adults and Libraries: A How-to-Do-It Manual*, has said that teens should wear road signs around their necks that read "under construction."[5] In truth, when working with teens, you never know who they will turn out to be and which of your words or actions will stick with them for life. But it is always your decision whether to help them on their journey or hold them back.

Why Teens Are the Way They Are (and How They Differ from Adults)

All of us who work in libraries were once young adults ourselves. However, for many of us it is difficult to remember what it was like to be a teenager. Take a moment to think back on your own adolescence:

Who were your best friends in junior high and high school?

What kind of clothes did you wear?

What did you like to do after school?

What kinds of books did you like to read? (Or did you like to read at all?)

Did you ever use the library when you were a teen? Why or why not?

It is important not to make the mistake of assuming that things are the same for today's teens as they were when you were growing up (see figure 1.1). Today's young adults have to

FIGURE 1.1 ▌ **Top 10 Changes Affecting Students since the 1960s**

1. The number of dysfunctional families has grown.
2. High technology has influenced school, work, and home life.
3. Children are threatened by crime, violence, and poverty.
4. Communities are changing and becoming more diverse.
5. The influence of the mass media has tightened its grip on children, giving them more knowledge at an earlier age.
6. Students question authority and shun traditional values and responsibilities.
7. A hurry-up society often lacks a sense of community.
8. Changing workplaces create demands for higher levels of literacy.
9. Knowledge about learning styles demands new kinds of education.
10. Peers exert a powerful influence on values.

SOURCE: Julia Stratton, *How Students Have Changed . . . A Call to Action* (Arlington, Va.: American Association of School Administrators, 1995).

According to a 1998 survey conducted by the Shell Oil Company and released by the U.S. Department of Education, the lives of teenagers are filled with pressures and issues that they must deal with in today's world. Although two-thirds of the high school students polled said their lives were somewhat tough, three-fourths of the students said their future looked promising.

Teens felt the most pressure about getting good grades (44%) and getting into college (32%). They were also concerned about fitting in socially (29%), using drugs and alcohol (19%), and being sexually active (13%).

The groups most likely to report difficulties were high school juniors, African Americans, girls, and those teens in single-parent households.

A significant minority of students think their friends have problems with drugs and alcohol (43%), academics (30%), family life (35%), school violence (32%), and not having enough to do outside of school (29%). For African American students, in particular, violence in school is the single biggest problem they identify (51%); high school students in the South also indicate that school violence is a serious problem (40%).

The majority of America's teens say they feel happy (93%), cared about (91%), confident (86%), and fortunate (84%). Seventy-three percent of teens who say their parents read to them very frequently feel confident they have made the right decisions in their choice of friends, compared to only 52 percent of teens who say their parents read to them infrequently.

For a more detailed report of this survey see the Shell Oil Web Site: http://www.countonshell.com/SOC/ShellPoll/TeensTalk/TeensIndex.html

deal with many issues, such as an increase in drug and alcohol use and teen violence, that were less pervasive in previous generations. However, adolescence has always been a time of change, experimentation, excitement, and uncertainty. Many of the emotions experienced by today's teens are the same ones that you felt when you were a teen yourself. Confronting someone else going through these familiar (if forgotten) changes may make dealing with adolescents difficult and even painful. Recognizing both the normal developmental changes of adolescence and the hidden source of one's reaction to them is a vital part of getting past personal irritations to provide good public service to a significant portion of the library's clientele.

Everyone has painful memories from their own teen years. Using patience and compassion when working with adolescents in libraries grants us the opportunity to help smooth the way for other people going through the same difficult passage that we have been through. Remembering all the cruelties of adolescence may inspire us to be that much kinder to the teens whom we encounter in the library.

Puberty is a time of rapid physical growth in the human life cycle, second in velocity only to the first two years of life. Unfortunately, physical growth occurs at different rates among people of the same age; it also happens simultaneously with all the other changes going on at different rates within the same individual. Thus, it is an easy mistake to expect a kid who looks mature to behave like an adult. Physical appearance in adolescence is highly deceptive and should not be used as a barometer of social and cognitive maturity (see figure 1.2).

The rapid physical growth of early adolescence generally leads to a period of clumsiness and exaggerated self-consciousness. Young people at this point are consumed with mastering a changed (and changing) body, wondering whether they are normal, and worrying

FIGURE 1.2   ▌ **Seven Developmental Needs of Young Adolescents**

1. Physical Activity
   - boundless energy and dreamy lethargy
   - growing bodies need time to move and relax
2. Competence and Achievement
   - self-conscious about themselves
   - need to do something well and receive admiration
   - chances to prove themselves
3. Self-Definition
   - need opportunities to explore widening world
   - reflect upon new experiences and their roles
4. Creative Expression
   - need to express new feelings and interests

   - helps them understand and accept themselves
5. Positive Social Interaction with Peers and Adults
   - need support, companionship, and criticism
   - relationships with those willing to share
6. Structure and Clear Limits
   - know and understand rules of the system
   - search for security is helped by boundaries
7. Meaningful Participation
   - need to express social and intellectual skills
   - gain a sense of responsibility

SOURCE: Patrick Jones, "Seven Developmental Needs of Young Adolescents" (A handout from Serving the Underserved, a seminar conducted by The Young Adult Library Services Association of the American Library Association, June 1994, in Miami, Florida). Based upon Gayle Dorman, *The Middle Grades Assessment Program: User's Manual* (Chapel Hill, N.C.: Center for Early Adolescence, 1981).

about the way everybody else is reacting to them. One of the ways they buffer themselves against all this self-consciousness is to use their friends as a barometer of change. It can also be difficult for teens to perceive these changes taking place in their friends before such change happens to them.

Adolescent self-consciousness may make teens hesitant to approach library staff for fear of calling attention to themselves because they think the staff will think they are stupid or because other people may look at or overhear them. Self-consciousness may also make them relatively inarticulate about what they need or want. A little extra personal attention by staff will go a long way toward overcoming these largely imaginary fears.

In many ways, adolescence is a middle ground between childhood and adulthood. Teenagers' bodies are beginning to resemble the bodies of adults, and many teens are intellectually eager to be treated with the credibility of adults. Yet they are still dependent on their parents for such basic needs as food, shelter, and financial support, and they lack the experience that

In a 1997 study of 2,000 teenagers, what did teens look forward to most when going back to school in the fall?

- 89% seeing friends after summer's end
- 84% meeting new people
- 71% looking forward to the social scene and parties
- 70% shopping for new clothes
- 67% looking forward to "learning new things"[6]

In a survey of girls in their senior year of high school in 1992, what life values were deemed "very important?"

- 90% being successful in work
- 80% having strong friendships
- 77% providing better opportunities for their own children
- 62% having leisure time
- 49% having children[7]

Why teens don't use libraries:

- 74% competition from other activities
- 38% lack of interest in library services, resources, programs
- 31% lack of knowledge about library services
- 13% lack of transportation
- 8% lack of school assignments requiring library services
- 3% neighborhood safety[8]

In a survey of high school seniors in 1992, what activities did they participate in during their after-school hours?

- 88% do things with friends
- 73% drive around
- 67% do things with a parent
- 29% work or hold a part-time job
- 24% use a personal computer
- 8% watch television[9]

comes with age. It can be very frustrating to be simultaneously dependent and independent during this time of life.

Socially, adolescence is the time when one separates from parents and moves into a degree of interdependence and engagement with the larger world outside the family. Friends at this age often provide a staging ground for the emerging social behaviors needed as adults.

Because of these strong friendships, adolescents often travel in groups, surrounding themselves protectively with others who can relate to their experiences. In fact, all the research into teens at risk makes clear that one of the signs that a young person is in trouble is the absence of friends; this is a more serious problem than the highly touted excessive dependence on the peer group. Learning how to make and keep friends outside the family is a normal and healthy part of growing up, one that is especially important for young adults. Any service attitude or policy that acknowledges this reality will go a long way toward giving good public service to young adults.

Who Serves Young Adults?

Regardless of whether your library has a young adult (YA) specialist on staff, it is everyone's responsibility to make sure that teens receive the same quality library service as all other patrons. Whether a young adult approaches the desk in the children's department, the reference department, or the young adult department, she or he should be treated with courtesy and assisted within the scope of that department's expertise. Referring all teens to a young adult specialist, regardless of the type of information that the teen is seeking, is not making good use of the library's resources. Nor is it sending a good message to the teen,

In a 1994 poll, what did teenagers say was their favorite leisure activity?

- 98% watch television
- 93% listen to CDs or tapes
- 81% talk on the telephone
- 80% "hang out" with friends
- 75% play sports
- 73% read magazines
- 69% watch rented videos
- 56% work on a hobby
- 48% go to the movies
- 33% visit library or museum
- 24% volunteer work[10]

who may get the impression that most staff members don't want to assist her or him.

For this reason, all public service staff members in a library should have a general understanding of how to serve young adults. Staff members who are particularly interested or skilled in serving young adults can share their knowledge by doing presentations at staff meetings and sharing articles of interest with their colleagues. Tips on serving teens may be included in a notebook to share with other librarians at public service desks. YALSA also maintains a list of trainers who are available to do more formal presentations on young adult services in libraries across the United States.

Treating the young adult as another human being in search of an answer will go a long way in gaining respect and keeping control at a focal point of the library. If a young adult is waiting in line while you help someone else, acknowledge the teen and say, "I'll be with you in a minute." Be sensitive to the exaggerated self-consciousness of many adolescents and be kind and patient. Never trivialize or ridicule their question or how it is asked. And keep your sense of humor. Your behavior will convey that young adults are a welcome part of your clientele, not only to them, but also to colleagues and other patrons.

Young Adult Librarians

Ideally, every library would have at least one young adult specialist whose primary job is to address the informational and recreational needs of teens in libraries. Studies have shown that youth services specialists, who are hired to serve both children and teens, spend only 22 percent of their time on young adult services.[11] It is likely that adult services specialists and others whose auxiliary focus is to serve YAs spend even less time and energy on services to teens. Excellent service to one quarter of the public library's population can be time-consuming and does warrant a full-time position or department of its own. However, many libraries are not able to employ a young adult librarian, and young adult services are frequently one of the first areas to be cut from public library budgets during lean times.

Generalists

If your library does not have a young adult librarian or young adult services department, it is all the more important to ensure that the needs of teens are being addressed in your library.

If young adult services are something that you are trying to juggle along with other job responsibilities, it is imperative that you set priorities and stick to them. Create a plan of service for young adults in your library and schedule time on a regular basis to implement your plan.

Because of the uncanny (but normal) ability of most adolescents to magnify a single unpleasant encounter in a library into full-blown egocentric anticipation of similar treatment in the future, consistently pleasant service is extremely important. A librarian who is not used to working with young adults is apt to become impatient and exasperated and may let it show. This can be damaging in several ways. The librarian may inhibit a shy teen who needs a question answered, and the incident may further block the young adult from wanting to use the library; after all, who wants to go where he or she is not wanted? The overall image of the library suffers as well. Several small incidents of perceived poor treatment may spread the word that the public library is not a nice place to visit.

How to Interact with Teens

Interacting with teens in the library should not be very different from interacting with any other client group. It is just a little more intense. When in doubt about how to act around a young adult, think how you would approach an adult in the same situation and give the teen the benefit of the doubt. If you are an effective librarian, you already possess the qualities necessary to be an effective young adult librarian, with a few possible exceptions.

Respect

Perhaps the most important characteristic of library services to young adults is a *respect* for teens and the willingness to help them access the materials they need. This means a willingness on your part to utilize whatever tools (such as interlibrary loan or online searching) are necessary to satisfy their requests. It also means taking their questions seriously, no matter how obvious or trivial their information needs may seem to you. If a teen comes into the library with his or her parent, address the teen directly, rather than asking the parent about the teen's needs.

Responsiveness

It is a mistake to assume that all young adults are alike. It is important to be responsive to the diverse needs of the community served through collection development, programming, and direct service. This means understanding the unique nature of adolescence and adolescents—the physical, cognitive, social, and emotional changes that teenagers are experiencing. It also means assessing the informational and recreational needs of the young adults in your community accurately and comprehensively. It is essential to communicate with the young adults, their parents, school library media specialists, and their teachers to determine their informational needs. You must also stay abreast of popular culture to understand young adult recreational needs.

Approachability

An effective librarian does not use the desk as a barrier, does not appear too busy for patrons to ask for assistance, and makes eye contact with patrons; in short, makes it clear that the staff is there to help people. This quality is particularly important when working with young adults who, almost by definition, are self-conscious and may be unsure of themselves.

Helpfulness

To be really effective with teens in the library, you may have to approach them directly to see if they need assistance. Many librarians find that it is more effective to ask young adults if they are finding what they need rather than asking if they need help. This avoids putting the teen in a position of feeling as if they don't know what they're doing. Once you have made patrons aware of your willingness to help, respect their response. Some teens may feel a sense of accomplishment by figuring things out for themselves, while others will undoubtedly be grateful for your assistance.

Patience and Persistence

When working with younger teens, patience is particularly important. You must remember that their nascent cognitive skills don't fully develop overnight and permanently. The thirteen-year-old who grasped the abstraction of a periodical index last week may have difficulty with it this week. Persistence may also be very helpful when trying to contact school library media specialists and teachers regarding homework assignments. But your patience and persistence will pay off and save you time and effort later.

Good Memory

As with any reference interaction, the ability to recall such information as current events and the names (or at least the location) of particularly helpful reference works is important. When working with young adults, it is important to be able to remember homework assignments and resources that were helpful. It is also useful to remember the names of YA patrons and their interests—the young girl who prefers science fiction to romance novels or the boy who devours biographies. Most teens are impressed if you recommend a book to them, and then ask them what they thought of it the next time you encounter them in the library.

Empathy

While empathy is helpful in dealing with any patron, it is especially important when interacting with young adults. If you can remember the awkwardness and self-consciousness, the questions and fears of your own teen years, you will be more effective when dealing with young adult patrons. What may seem to be a minor problem or a trivial request to you could seem like the "end of the world" to a teenager. Understanding the degree to which their "acting out" behavior is a manifestation of their insecurity will also help you deal with them more fairly.

Be Yourself

Since young adults often view adults as authority figures, it is sometimes helpful to use a relaxed and informal style when interacting with them. It is important not to try to act too "cool," however. Teens can spot a phony from a mile away, and if they sense that you are trying too hard to relate to them, your attempt to put them at ease may backfire. Most importantly, be yourself when relating to young adults. Ask questions if you don't understand what they are talking about. Teens are often flattered when adults ask their opinions about things, and you may learn a lot from talking openly with them about their interests and how to serve them better in the library.

Open-Mindedness

Since adolescence is a time of emerging independence, many teens express their newly discovered identity through nontraditional dress and grooming. Try to put their appearance aside when working with teens in the library. You should extend as much courtesy to a teen with a pink mohawk as you would to a businessman in a three-piece suit. Also, do not anticipate problems that don't exist. A group of teens entering the library does not always evolve into a behavior problem. Respond to specific situations, not to anticipated stereotypical behavior of a certain age group.

Sense of Humor

When working with young adults, it is important not to take yourself too seriously. Being flexible is essential in establishing smooth relationships with teens. Often, the key to effective work with teenagers is not to try harder, but to try softer. If you relax, you will put them at ease, which will help greatly in your interaction with them.

NOTES

1. Ana Marie Cox, "Wasted on the Young," FEED (http://www. feedmag.com) July 10, 1998.

2. Shell Oil Company, Teens Talk to America, 1999. Available at http://www.countonshell.com/SOC/ShellPoll/TeensTalk/Teens Index.html

3. U.S. Department of Education, National Center for Education Statistics, *Library Statistics of Colleges and Universities,* various years; and Integrated Postsecondary Education Data System, "Academic Library Survey."

4. Terry Stevens Ayers, in *Youth Participation in School and Public Libraries: It Works,* by the Youth Participation Committee of the Young Adult Library Services Association, a Division of the American Library Association, ed. Caroline A. Caywood (Chicago: American Library Association, 1995), xi.

5. Patrick Jones, *Connecting Young Adults and Libraries: A How-to-Do-It Manual*, rev. ed. (New York: Neal-Schuman, 1997).

6. Excerpted from Lisa C. Wemett, "Young Adults by the Numbers," *Statistics Shared in "Family Feud" and Their Sources* from Teenage Research Unlimited, Northbrook, Ill. Press release posted on the Web site, www.teenresearch.com/school97.html, "What Back-to-School Really Means to Teens."

7. Excerpted from Lisa C. Wemett, "Young Adults by the Numbers," *Statistics Shared in "Family Feud" and Their Sources* from U.S. Department of Education, National Center for Education Statistics, "National Longitudinal Study" First Follow up Study, "High School and Beyond," Youth Indicators 1996, Indicator #55, "Values." http://nces.ed.gov/pubs/yi

8. U.S. Department of Education, Office of Educational Research and Improvement, National Center for Education Statistics, *Services and Resources for Children and Young Adults in Public Libraries* (Washington, D.C.: U.S. Government Printing Office, 1995), 54–55.

9. Excerpted from Lisa C. Wemett, "Young Adults by the Numbers," *Statistics Shared in "Family Feud" and Their Sources* from U.S. Department of Education, National Center for Education Statistics, High School and Beyond, Second Follow up Study, Youth Indicators 1996, Indicator #40, "After School Activities." http://nces.ed.gov/pubs/yi

10. Excerpted from Lisa C. Wemett, "Young Adults by the Numbers," *Statistics Shared in "Family Feud" and Their Sources* from Peter Zollo, *Wise Up to Teens* (1995), p. 88. Teenage Research Unlimited Teenage Marketing and Lifestyle Study 1994. http://www.teenresearch.com

11. U.S. Department of Education, Office of Educational Research and Improvement, National Center for Education Statistics, *Services and Resources for Children and Young Adults in Public Libraries* (Washington, D.C.: U.S. Government Printing Office, 1995).

2

Youth Participation

The easiest way to serve young adults in libraries is to get them involved in the planning process. Although it is a common misconception that it is too time-consuming to set up a Teen Advisory Board, involving teens in library planning can actually save time by quickly identifying the most pressing needs and avoiding the trial and error that often comes with collection development and programming for this age group. Youth participation can be as simple as using teen volunteers and pages in the library or reserving a position on the library Board of Trustees or Foundation Board for a teen representative.

In *Youth Participation in School and Public Libraries: It Works*, the most successful youth participation programs were found to meet the following criteria:

> They encourage the participation of all segments of the youth population, not just "troublemakers" or high achievers.
>
> They engage the youth in activities that are challenging and interesting to the participants and allow them to exercise initiative, responsibility, and control over the activities.
>
> They provide the youth with adequate training and supervision to perform their tasks well.[1]

YALSA's Youth Participation Committee meets at every ALA convention to explore ways to encourage youth participation in libraries and in professional activities (see figure 2.1). It also hosts YA-YAAC, an electronic discussion list created for library youth groups and their facilitators to share ideas.

Surveys

Surveys are an easy way to solicit teen input about library services. Surveys may be conducted (with permission) in schools or public libraries and can be written or verbal, formal or informal. Surveys may be used to determine appropriate directions for young adult services as a whole or to assist with planning more specific aspects of young adult services, such as generating program ideas and determining local YA reading interests to assist with collection development.

FIGURE 2.1   ▍   **YALSA Guidelines for Youth Participation in Libraries**

Projects involving youth should have the following characteristics:

> be centered on issues of real interest and concern to youth
>
> have the potential to benefit people other than those directly involved
>
> allow for youth input from the planning stage forward
>
> focus on some specific, doable tasks
>
> receive adult support and guidance but avoid adult domination
>
> allow for learning and development of leadership and group work skills
>
> contain opportunities for training and for discussion of progress made and problems encountered
>
> give evidence of youth decisions being implemented
>
> avoid exploitation of youth for work that benefits the agency rather than the young adults
>
> seek to recruit participants on a regular basis
>
> plan for staff time, funds, administrative support, transportation, and so on before launching a project
>
> show promise of becoming an ongoing, long-term activity.

SOURCE: Youth Participation Committee of the Young Adult Library Services Association, American Library Association, *Youth Participation in School and Public Libraries: It Works*, ed. Caroline A. Caywood (Chicago: YALSA, 1995), 5.

Before conducting a survey, determine what it is that you want to know. If you are already working with a group of teens in your library, you might want to involve them in the process of creating the survey. Questions should be specific and clear. Sample surveys can be found in many YA professional publications (see figure 2.2).

Students can also be involved in the process of conducting the survey. Young adults can ask questions of their peers when they visit the library or assist with distributing written surveys

FIGURE 2.2 ▌ **Young Adult Library Survey**

1. How many items (books, magazines, tapes, etc.) did you check out today? _____

2. Were you looking for anything particular in the library? yes   no

   If you were just browsing, skip to question 3.

   If you were looking for particular things, please list them here:

   a. _____

       Did you find it?   yes   no

       Was it for school? yes   no

   b. _____

       Did you find it?   yes   no

       Was it for school? yes   no

   c. _____

       Did you find it?   yes   no

       Was it for school? yes   no

   If you were looking for more than three things, please list the others on the back.

3. If you were just browsing and not looking for anything special, did you find anything interesting?   yes   no

4. Did you come to the library for some completely different reason, such as attending a program or meeting a friend or using the rest room?   yes   no

5. How old are you? _____

6. Is there anything else you want to tell us about the library? You may write on the back of the page if you want to.

Thank you for answering our questions today! Please leave this form in the marked box when you leave the library.

SOURCE: Virginia A. Walter, *Output Measures and More: Planning and Evaluating Public Library Services for Young Adults* (Chicago and London: American Library Association, 1995), appendix B.

in the schools. Teens can also assist in compiling the data collected in the survey and in disseminating the results.

It is important to follow through on the results of your survey. Purchase materials that teens indicate they are interested in using. Plan programs based on their identified areas of interest. Rather than interpreting any comments as criticism, take advantage of the advice that you receive to make changes that will improve your library's service to young adults.

Focus Groups

If your library is considering creating a new service, such as a young adult collection or YA summer reading program, a focus group can be helpful in effective planning. Inviting a small group of teens to participate in the planning process can provide insights that librarians often ignore when designing services for young adults.

An effective focus group will consist of teens who are representative of the audience that you hope to target for a new service. Attention should be paid to age and gender balance, as well as to representation from various schools, socioeconomic levels, and ethnic groups in your community. You may want to create more than one focus group to examine a particular issue to account for group dynamics. Participants in a focus group can be handpicked or recruited through advertising in the local newspaper and through the schools.

Dates for focus group meetings should take into consideration the schedules and time commitments of the participants, and meeting time should be used wisely. Having an agenda prepared before the meeting can ensure that all aspects of an issue will be discussed and help minimize digressions.

Invite students to participate in a focus group during the planning process of a new service, not after decisions have been made. Make clear to the students that their opinions will be considered in implementing the service, but that not all of their suggestions may be feasible to implement.

Solicit opinions from the focus group about all aspects of the proposed service, and give students the opportunity to brainstorm situations that may not have been considered by the library.

Focus groups should generally meet for a specific period of time. Often only one or two meetings may be necessary to acquire the information necessary to begin a new service. Follow-up meetings of a focus group, after the service is in place or after a short-term project has been completed, allow students to provide feedback on whether the project was a success and what can be done to improve it.

Focus groups are an excellent way to plan young adult services. Teens often appreciate the opportunity to be involved in the planning process. Their involvement usually will cost the library no more than the price of refreshments at the meetings and the acknowledgement of their services. As with any volunteers, it is courteous to publicly thank your focus group participants, either orally or in writing, for the service they have provided to the library.

Junior Friends Groups

Like their adult counterparts, the primary function of Junior Friends of the Library groups is to raise money for the library and increase awareness of the library within the community.

Information about forming Junior Friends groups can be obtained from Friends of the Library—U.S.A. (FOLUSA), 1420 Walnut Street, Suite 450, Philadelphia, PA 19102. Telephone 1-800-9FOLUSA. www.folusa.com

Junior Friends may team up with the adult Friends of the Library group for their traditional fund-raisers such as book sales or bake sales, or create other avenues of fund-raising for the library. Junior Friends may be supervised by the young adult librarian or another library staff member or by an adult volunteer, following the adult Friends' model (see figure 2.3).

Fund-raising opportunities for teens are as varied as the ideas they can come up with and may include charging admission for programs such as dances and concerts that fall outside of the scope of regular library activities, or convincing a local bookstore or retail establishment to donate a portion of its proceeds to the library on a particular day or evening.

Junior Friends groups can also provide nonmonetary services such as creating a library newsletter or doing volunteer work in the library or in the community as representatives of the library. Such activities can raise awareness of library services and garner goodwill in the community.

FIGURE 2.3 | **Organizing a Junior Friends of the Library Group**

1. Choose goals for the group. These could include motivating people to use the library, providing physical help in the library, decorating, helping with story hours, and so on, or a combination of these. Parents usually serve as adult leaders or as members of the Friends. Staff members cannot be expected to assume this responsibility. However, they should be involved with program ideas, project ideas, publicity, and scheduling.

2. Target the age range, based on availability of adult sponsors. They can include grades K-1, 2-4, 5-8, or 9-12. Start with a workable group; you can always expand.

3. Set dues, even if very low. It increases the importance of the group. The adult Friends may set aside funds for Junior Friends, especially in the formative stages, and provide refreshments, membership cards, and so on.

4. Hold an organizational meeting. Depending on the age group, present bylaws and discuss potential programs and projects.

5. Select or elect officers, if desirable.

6. Appoint committees, involving everyone in at least one. Suggested committees include Program, Projects, Membership, and Publicity.

7. Develop potential projects. Possibilities for Junior Friends are sponsoring Junior Great Books programs, decorating for holidays, clipping for files, sponsoring various contests, presenting book reviews for peers, helping with story hours, and contributing to community festivities.

8. Keep business portions of meetings brief.

9. Keep work and fun projects in balance.

10. Do not let adults assume responsibility for planning. Members should make decisions with the assistance of adults, who should watch that students not plan projects that are too ambitious.

SOURCE: Friends of Libraries U.S.A. "Fact Sheet #5, How to Organize a Junior Friends of the Library Group."

Teen Advisory Boards

One of the easiest ways to start young adult programs is to involve those students who are already library users. Invite regular patrons, teen library volunteers, and pages to an introductory meeting and ask them to spread the word and bring their friends. The schools also provide an excellent forum to publicize your advisory board: work with the school library media specialist to post a notice in the halls of the school or in the school or public newspaper or write a letter to teachers asking them to nominate students who might be interested in participating. Some schools will allow you to submit an announcement to be read over the intercom system at the beginning of the school day or by individual teachers in their classes. If the success of your Teen Advisory Board (TAB) is greater than you anticipated, you may need to develop a way to narrow down the pool of applicants to those who will best contribute to your organization. An application and interview process might be considered if the number of students who wish to be involved exceeds the number you can comfortably supervise in a meeting. Some libraries that find themselves in this situation create multiple teen groups, divided by age, by school, or by areas of interest.

Once you have established a Teen Advisory Board, it is important to involve the students in the coordination of their own meetings. Ask the teens how they would like the meetings to be structured, when and how often they would like to meet, and what kinds of activities they would like to participate in. Provide the students with a list of possibilities to get them thinking about ways they can contribute to the library, but allow them the opportunity to express their own ideas as well (see figure 2.4).

It may be helpful to create a mission statement for your Teen Advisory Board with the help of its members. The board should also establish standards of behavior for the meetings. For example, the Youth Advisory Board in Bloomington, Indiana, uses a rubber chicken to designate whose turn it is to speak at a meeting. At the beginning of each year, you may want to have the students set goals or priorities for the Teen Advisory Board to accomplish. At the end of the year, have the students complete an evaluation that reviews their accomplishments, highlights their achievements, and suggests areas for improvement in the following year.

For a sample of Teen Advisory Board organization, see "By-Laws for the Louisville Public Library Teen Advisory Board" on page 91.

Serving refreshments at your meetings may make them more appealing, especially during the early stages before the group has taken on a life of its own. Creating an agenda for each meeting based on the activities that the teens have decided upon can help you stay on task. If your group decides to

FIGURE 2.4 ▌ **Sample Teen Advisory Board Activities**

Plan programs

Visit local bookstores to buy books for the library

Assist in collection development by reviewing journals and recommending titles

Create displays

Educate librarians about teen reading interests and recreational activities

Plan get-togethers with teens from other agencies that serve youth in your community

Have get-to-know-each-other activities to create a sense of belonging in the group

Talk about books!

Write and perform murder mysteries

Create a newsletter for the library

Attend professional conferences, ALA or your state convention

Read to younger children, in hospitals, and so on

Plan YA summer reading or have teens assist with children's summer reading

Create a video of the library from a teen's perspective

Create or contribute to the library's Web site

Create reading lists or special collections of books recommended by teens

Invite other TABs to your library to share ideas at a youth participation conference

Host a sleepover at the library for teens or for younger children run by teens

elect officers, involve the president or vice president of your TAB in planning and running the meetings and in creating minutes to be mailed to members afterward.

Be sure to promote the accomplishments of your Teen Advisory Board within both the library and the community. Remember to honor your TAB members whenever other library volunteers are being recognized. Small rewards such as food, field trips, and simple gratitude and praise can go a long way toward repaying the teens who help you do your job, and a successful Teen Advisory Board should do just that.

Youth participants can assist libraries with programming, collection development, marketing, fund-raising, and advocacy,

For me, the Teen Library Council has been both a way to meet kids my own age I share some things in common with (i.e., no cable) and a way to get more kids interested in reading. It's also opened me up to different genres and authors that I might not have otherwise checked out that were suggested to me by various TLC members. I hope I have been able to give to the program as much as I've received from it.[2]

as well as provide the opportunity for librarians to serve as mentors to youth. The young adults in turn gain a better understanding of how the library works and what resources it provides. They also learn respect for other students who don't necessarily share the same age, background, and interests as they do, and they learn to work as a team to accomplish a goal. Additionally, they will develop a sense of responsibility and pride in public service that will serve them and their communities as they grow into adult citizens. And, perhaps most importantly, both the students and the librarians should have fun.

NOTES

1. Youth Participation Committee of the Young Adult Library Services Association, a Division of the American Library Association, *Youth Participation in School and Public Libraries: It Works*, ed. Caroline A. Caywood (Chicago: YALSA, 1995), 3.

2. Adam Tierney, Carmel Clay (Ind.) Public Library Teen Library Council member, 1998.

3

Planning for Young Adult Services

If you are interested in establishing young adult services in your library for the first time or expanding services that currently exist, your first step is to "sell the idea" to administration. *Output Measures and More: Planning and Evaluating Public Library Services for Young Adults* lists possible selling points to help persuade administrators that service to young adults should be a priority in your library.[1] It also contains valuable information about how to apply the planning and role-setting process to library services for young adults as well as detailed instructions on measuring services that you already have in place.

In addition to explaining the "whys" of serving YAs, you need to know the "hows" of meeting the needs of this age group in the library. "Focus Questions for Administrators," developed by Judy Druse, a curriculum/media librarian at Washburn University in Topeka, Kansas, helps you understand the issues to address with your library administration to pave the way for successful young adult services (see figure 3.1).

Make sure that young adult services are represented in your library's planning process. The Public Library Association's guidebook *Planning for Results* provides a detailed overview of the planning process that may be applied to young adult services as well.[2] It provides information about identifying needs, assessing resources, and establishing goals and objectives. It also recommends involving members of the

FIGURE 3.1

Focus Questions for Administrators

Questions to ask administrators, managers, and supervisors to help them evaluate their library services to YAs:

Have you assigned the best person available to work with YAs? (This is not necessarily the children's librarian.)

1. Policies

Does your library have a written policy that supports the Library Bill of Rights and its interpretations that deal with equal access for YAs?

Does your library have a written policy on disruptive behavior that applies to all library users?

Are other policies in existence that hinder services or do not meet the developmental needs of YAs?

2. Training

Has your staff been trained to handle disruptive behavior in compliance with library policy?

Has your staff (right down to the custodian) been trained on understanding YAs?

Does everyone on staff understand library policies and limits, as well as staff proper actions and reactions?

3. Youth Participation

Are YAs actively involved in planning services and policies applicable to YAs?

Do you know what the YAs in your area expect from their library?

What would YAs like you to do that you're not doing?

4. Trustees and Friends

Do your trustees and Friends group understand why it is important to serve YAs?

Do they have suggestions about how to encourage library use by YAs?

5. Location of YA Area

Is your YA area located close to quiet study areas or the front door and circulation desk?

6. Library Documents

Is there a line item in the budget for YA expenditures?

Is there a collection development plan for YA materials?

Do the words "young adult" show up in library documents such as the annual report?

7. Mission, Vision, Goals, Objectives

Does your library have a mission or vision statement and is there a parallel statement for services to YAs?

What are the library's goals and objectives for serving YAs?

8. Evaluation and Assessment

How do you evaluate the success of your services for YAs?

Do you use the assessments delineated in *Output Measures and More?*

SOURCE: Judy Druse, "Focus Questions for Administrators" (from the manual for Serving the Underserved II, a seminar conducted by the Young Adult Library Services Association of the American Library Association, January 1996, in San Antonio, Texas), 3-16.

community (including young adults!) as well as library staff and administrators in a planning committee to develop a vision, mission, and service responses for the library:

The Library Strives to Achieve These Results
 (that meet community needs)
 Vision

By Providing These Services
 Service Responses

Which Are Summarized in These Words
That Are Meaningful to the Community
 Mission

It is the responsibility of the Young Adult Librarian to ensure that the needs of young adults are addressed in these statements.

YALSA has developed a list of young adult competencies that will help you evaluate the skills of the staff members who will be working with young adults in your library or can help you set standards for hiring new staff to work with young adults. See "Young Adults Deserve the Best: YALSA Competencies for Librarians Serving Youth" on page 97.

After receiving administrative support to develop young adult services in your library and assigning competent staff to work with teens, you should gather information about the young adults in your community and assess the current services available for this age group.

Be sure to involve young adults in this process. Although demographic information obtained from the local newspapers, Chamber of Commerce, and the schools may be useful in identifying some aspects of the young adult population in your community, talking to kids (through focus groups, surveys, or other informal methods) will reveal more subtle needs and interests.

Contact other agencies serving youth within your community, such as churches, youth groups, parks and recreational departments, clubs, and sports teams, to find out what services are already available for teens. This will provide the opportunity to work cooperatively with other agencies serving teens in your area. Avoiding duplication of services will reduce competition for attendance at your programs.

Once you have analyzed the information you have gathered, you can create a plan of action to meet the needs of teens that are not being addressed elsewhere.

Creating a Young Adult Services Plan

If your library has never had young adult services, or if you are substantially revising your library's YA program, you may want to create a formal Young Adult Services Plan to present to the library board and administration as well as to the staff and community. Your plan should begin by defining what you mean by "young adult." YALSA defines young adults as people between the ages of twelve and eighteen. This definition varies widely from library to library. Your library may want to focus specifically on a more narrow age range within this population, or extend the age range up or even (as some bookstores have done) down. Your YA plan should include your rationale for providing library services to young adults as well as a detailed description of what those services would entail. It might also include a timeline for accomplishing each proposed segment of your YA plan.

For one example of a YA plan, see "Plan for Library Services to Young Adults" on page 102.

Young Adult Goals and Objectives

After you have determined your young adult services vision, mission, and long-range plan, the next step in the planning process is to create specific goals and objectives that follow from these statements. Your goals should be broad and far-reaching; they should identify what you are trying to achieve in providing library services to young adults. Objectives explain the specific steps you plan to take to achieve these goals (see figure 3.2).

Action Plan To further help you with your day-to-day planning, you might want to create an action plan that outlines the specific methods you will use to achieve your goals and objectives. Your action plan may take the form of annual goals, which contain measurable steps and target dates of accomplishment for each task. It may be helpful to organize your action plan according to identified areas of priority for your library or for young

FIGURE 3.2 ▌ **Sample Young Adult Long-Term Goals and Objectives**

1. Identify young adult needs appropriate for library support

   through encouraging youth participation, soliciting input from junior high and high school students, having authentic reference interactions with teenagers, and carrying out effective use of technology and ongoing professional development.

2. Implement effective strategies to meet the needs of young adults

   through a collection of popular materials in a variety of formats and through programs that present a wide range of views on current and historical issues and can be evaluated using quantitative and qualitative output measures.

3. Effectively and creatively promote and publicize the full range of young adult materials and services we offer

   through library publications, outreach, and other public relations efforts.

4. Advocate within the library and the community for the information rights and needs of young adults

   through cooperative involvement with local schools and other agencies that serve teenagers.

SOURCE: Renée J. Vaillancourt, "Young Adult Long Term Goals / Objectives," Carmel Clay (Ind.) Public Library, November 1995.

adult services in your library. Your action plan should take into account the time and staff you have to achieve your goals. Steps may be rolled over from one year to the next if not accomplished, but it is better to set reasonable goals than to "bite off more than you can chew." (See figure 3.3.)

Although your young adult plan, goals and objectives, and action plan will identify the direction your library is heading in regard to young adult services, the most important step in the process is the implementation of your plan. Setting specific and measurable goals and keeping to an established timeline will help you keep on track with your vision for young adult services. The planning process will also provide you with a framework for evaluation once your goals have been accomplished.

Evaluation

Be sure to include young adults in your evaluation process. Evaluations may be conducted using a formal process (written evaluation forms or focus group follow-up meetings) or by

FIGURE 3.3 ▌ **Sample Young Adult Action Plan**

Collection

Develop recommended reading list for seventh and eighth grade students by May 15.

Seek YA input (through TAB, surveys, reference encounters) on genre labeling of fiction to assist teens in finding the type of books they like to read by August 15.

Computer Technology

Automate summer reading program registration and volunteer scheduling by May 1.

With TAB assistance, improve library's YA Web page to include links more pertinent to YA interests and needs, and update content by September 1.

Management

Continue to increase awareness of young adult services through in-service trainings by February 15, and articles in the staff newsletter in June and September.

Outreach

Establish book and movie discussion program in conjunction with the high school library youth group during September through December.

Professional Development

Submit article on successful murder mystery program to professional library publications by April 15.

Attend at least one professional development session on Intellectual Freedom issues by August 1.

Programming

Increase high school student participation in library-sponsored summer activities by promoting summer reading and other events during school visits to all classes in May and through publicity at local teen hangouts and in the local media.

Plan two new programs for middle school students in April and October.

Teen Advisory Board

Establish a Junior Teen Advisory Board for junior high school students to accommodate the increased demand for student participation by August 30.

SOURCE: Adapted from Renée J. Vaillancourt, "Young Adult Services Goals 1998," Carmel Clay (Ind.) Public Library, January 1998.

simply reviewing the success of your services and observing areas that need improvement. Jotting down notes to keep in your file will ensure that you address any shortcomings if you decide to repeat a program or make changes in an ongoing service. It is important to view negative feedback as an opportunity to learn and grow rather than as a sign of failure. It is estimated that 10 percent of an audience will find something to complain about if given the opportunity to evaluate a service. This does not mean that the opinions of this 10 percent of the population should be ignored or obsessed about, but rather that they should be kept in perspective and balanced with the opinions of the other 90 percent of your population. Also, evaluation should be seen as an ongoing process. After a service is implemented, evaluated, and revised, it should be evaluated again and revised again until it has reached an optimum level of success. If this process is viewed as evolution rather than a tedious series of trial and error, it will allow staff and patrons to benefit from every step along the way rather than simply striving toward the final goal.

NOTES

1. Virginia A. Walter, *Output Measures and More: Planning and Evaluating Public Library Services for Young Adults* (Chicago: American Library Assn., 1995).

2. *Planning for Results: A Public Library Transformation Process* (Chicago: American Library Assn., 1998).

Creating a Young Adult Space

As with other aspects of young adult services, the easiest way to plan for a young adult area in your building is to involve teens in the process (see figure 4.1). Bring architectural and interior design magazines to a Teen Advisory Board meeting and have members mark layouts and furnishings that catch their eye with Post-its on which they jot down what they like about the picture. Take a group of teens on a field trip to the mall and see what kinds of retail environments they are drawn to. Pay special attention to details like lighting, signage, and displays. Also look at how the mall takes advantage of empty space—wider aisles create a more relaxed browsing environment, for example. Visit local bookstores with a substantial teen patronage. Observe how they arrange furniture to create a cozy living room atmosphere (and while you're there, pay attention to what kinds of books your teens are looking at—it might not be the standard YA fare you expect).

Location

Several factors should be considered when choosing a location for a young adult area. In a recent electronic discussion, one librarian said that the most important thing her Teen Advisory Board wanted in a young adult area was a space where they

FIGURE 4.1 ▍ **Survey Says . . .**

As part of the adolescent literature classwork component of her MLS in library science and instructional technology at Southern Connecticut State University in 1996, Miriam Neiman conducted an informal survey of twenty-four adolescents between the ages of ten and seventeen on the topic "What Do YAs Want in Their Ideal YA Section of the Library?" Here's what they said:

50% of the student-created floor plans partitioned the area into a study section and a casual reading section.

58% chose rectangular tables for studying.

79% wanted computers for research and recreational resources.

54% wanted carpeting or a rug so they could sit on the floor.

83% of the space designs included armchairs or recliners, often grouped side by side.

79% included a sofa or love seat, or both.

38% included beanbag chairs.

Nearly all respondents wanted the YA section "as far as possible from the children's area!"

Responses emphasized comfort and privacy.

Responses were contradictory about noise vs. quiet, music, and whether food should be allowed in the area.

SOURCE: Miriam Neiman, "What Do YAs Want in Their Ideal YA Section of the Library?" (adolescent literature course survey) Southern Connecticut State University, 1996.

wouldn't feel like they were bothering everyone around them. Because of the tendency for teens to "travel in packs," the young adult area should be situated in a location where talking teenagers will not be terribly disruptive. If you do not have a soundproof room available for this purpose, a location close to the circulation desk or lobby would make sense, since those tend to be fairly busy, noisy areas of the library.

On the other hand, many young adults are looking for a study space when they come to the library. Some have no quiet place to study at home and just need an individual carrel for several hours on a regular basis. Others need or want to study in groups where they can interact. The solution may be to divide your young adult area into one space where maximum quiet is enforced and another area where talking is allowed. If space is limited, you may want to consider the possibility of locating your young adult area close to individual or group study rooms that could be insulated against the sounds of the more noisy areas surrounding them. If the layout of your library will not accommodate quiet study and talking in the same space, consider placing your young adult area on the way to a quieter area such as the reference department. This will serve the double purpose of attracting into the area young adults who are on their way to doing more serious research if your YA area doesn't contain research materials.

Another area it would make sense to have your young adult space border would be the audiovisual (AV) department. Since many teens are drawn to audiovisual formats, placing the YA area next to the AV department is likely to enhance the use of both collections. If your library is fortunate enough to have a snack bar or coffee shop, it would also be wise to consider locating the YA collection near that area. Because of the rapid physical growth of adolescents, teens eat a lot. You might also want to discuss this fact with administration when determining your library's policy of allowing food and drink in the building.

Ideally, your young adult area should have a feeling of seclusion, although it should be located near a highly trafficked path in the library. Most importantly, it should not be located next to the children's department. Many young adolescents are just beginning to establish their own identity and resent being perceived as children.

In an average week, an American teenager consumes:

2.3	candy bars
8.3	sticks of gum
9.8	soft drinks
2.7	fast-food purchases
3.6	salty snacks[1]

Layout

If you think about the sanctity of a teenager's bedroom, it is easy to extrapolate that YAs like to have a space in the library they can consider their own. Therefore, the layout of your young adult area should clearly define the boundaries of the area, either by using bookshelves and other furnishings to form "walls" or by creating the space in an enclosed room. It is important to remember to create some means of visual supervision, however. Intimate cul-de-sacs pose inevitable problems because young adults think they are unobserved and become oblivious to the effect of their behavior on others. Most teens also like a cozy, living-room type setup. Furniture should be arranged in clusters to accommodate teenagers' affinity for discussion.

Since many teens are dependent on adults for transportation, and also because they are curious about what their peers are up to, it is useful to provide large windows in the young adult area, preferably facing the street or parking lot so that teens can wait for their rides in the area. A window seat is ideal, since it combines the functionality of a window with the coziness of a couch.

The young adult area should have clear signage indicating where it is and where various collections are housed within it. Neon signs are popular as well as eye-catching. Don't assume that "Young Adult" is the best way to name the area. Many teens don't know what the term "young adult" refers to. Consider inviting teens to give input about an appropriate name. Lining the outer walls of the area with magazines, paperbacks, or other displays of popular materials will also help draw teens in (see figure 4.2).

FIGURE 4.2 ▮ **One Example of a YA Floor Plan**

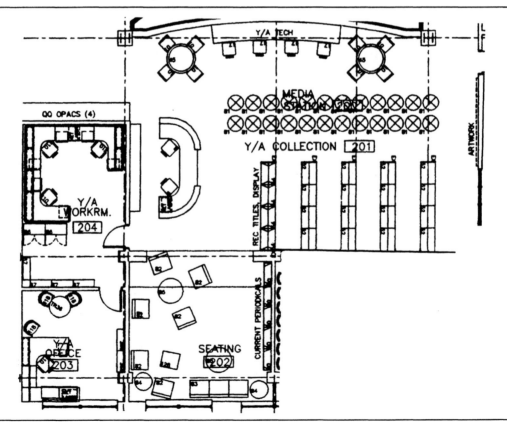

Courtesy of Carmel Clay (Ind.) Public Library and Meyer Scherer & Rockcastle, Ltd.

Since many teens look for books by genre, it might be worth considering shelving "bookstore style" within the young adult area. The catalogers won't like it, but teens will appreciate being able to go to specific areas to find mysteries, science fiction, and other popular genres.

Also, keep in mind the age group you are trying to target. If you hope to attract both older and younger teens to your area, you might want to consider designing the space so that materials for older teens aren't directly adjacent to or interfiled with materials for younger teens. In the same way that junior high students often resent being grouped with elementary school children, high school students are frequently sensitive to being affiliated with middle school students.

See figure 4.3 for a plan of an ideal library center designed by teens.

FIGURE 4.3

Youth Career/Recreation Center

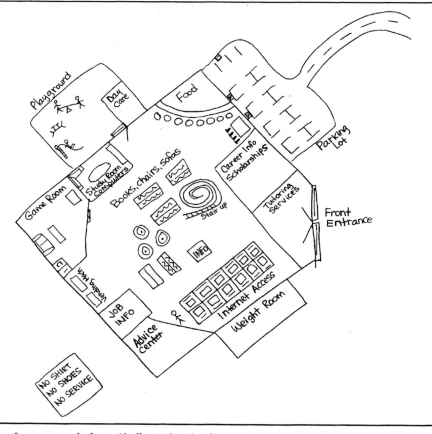

A focus group of young people from Cholla High School in Tucson, Arizona, created this illustration of an area they wanted to see in their library. Courtesy of Tucson-Pima Public Library, Tucson, Arizona

Furniture

Since teens often locate materials by browsing, spinning racks are good options for shelving paperbacks. The paperback spinners can also be situated to create "walls" that can be browsed from both sides to enclose your young adult area. There should be ample space for special displays and enough room on each bookshelf for face-out shelving to help "sell" books by their cover art.

In keeping with the "living room" environment, comfortable furniture, including durable couches, chairs, and coffee tables, should be included. Some libraries also provide special furnishings such as beanbag and butterfly chairs or tables with game boards embedded in the top. Although these are sure to be popular with young adults, make sure the furniture you buy for the young adult area is designed for heavy use. Teens are apt to put their feet on tables, hang legs over chair arms, and slouch on couches. If you already have furniture not designed for those who use the area, try to make the best of a difficult situation by establishing clear rules of behavior and enforcing them equitably. Ask the kids to help formulate fair rules that keep the furnishings functional for everybody.

If you are able to section off a quiet area within your YA space, that area should contain individual study carrels as well as small tables for partner or small-group study.

When designing your young adult area, you will also need to consider how it will be staffed and provide a desk or table space for reference and readers' advisory service if it will be staffed on a regular basis. The staff desk should be in a visible and accessible location, but not so close to the other furnishings that teens feel that their space is being invaded. Ideally, the staff desk would be located against a wall or in office space that is clearly visible from all other areas of the department.

Technology

When designing your young adult area, it is important to plan for the technological equipment that will be used in the area. The area should have at least one **OPAC** so that patrons can search for materials. If your library has a local area network (**LAN**), networked PCs or terminals should be located in the young adult area. A stand-alone PC can house **CD-ROMs** of educational and recreational interest to teens or provide word processing opportunities. If Internet access is available elsewhere in the building, it should be available to teens as well.

The number of computer stations that you have in your YA area will depend on the degree of usage. Young adults should not be expected to wait to use resources any more than other patrons should. As a general rule, if your library is not limited by funding, plan to provide enough PCs or terminals so that patrons do not have to wait longer than fifteen or thirty minutes to access electronic resources. This may mean adding additional stations as word spreads about your resources and their popularity increases.

A photocopy machine is practical to have in the YA area, particularly if you have a reference collection of books that are frequently used for assignments. This will not only provide patrons with a convenient means of copying the information they need, but may also cut down on the number of books that are stolen or mutilated.

Some libraries also provide a CD player and other AV equipment for teens to listen to music within the young adult area. Depending on how your building is set up, you could have music playing softly through speakers in the YA area, or allow patrons to check out cordless headphones to listen to tapes or CDs while they browse your collection. Stations to preview software or videos could also be set up, if space and funding permit.

Decor

If you want your YA space to be attractive to teens, it is essential to involve teens in the process of decorating. Artistically talented YAs could be invited to paint a mural on the wall of the area or to help design how it will be decorated. Hanging posters on the walls allows you to attract teens by using the latest pop icons without running the risk of dating the area by incorporating more permanent images of such passing trends.

Providing a bulletin board allows teens the opportunity to express themselves without damaging permanent fixtures and also allows you to provide information about other community agencies that offer services to teens. Some libraries also exhibit rotating collections of young adult art work or host contests for teens to create wall decorations for the young adult area.

An excellent form of ongoing evaluation for your young adult area is to provide a suggestion box in which teens can provide ideas for collection development, program topics, and even how to improve your newly designed young adult space!

NOTE

1. Herbert Buchsbaum, "The American Teenager by the Numbers," *Scholastic Update*, January 14, 1994, 8.

5

The Young Adult Collection

The focus of your YA collection should follow from your library's mission and service responses and your young adult services plan, goals, and objectives. For example, a library whose service responses include current topics and titles would have a YA collection that features recreational books and media, and possibly even board games; a library whose primary service response is formal learning support would have more curriculum-based materials. It is certainly possible and often desirable to combine popular materials with materials for reference and homework support within your young adult area. The important thing is that the decision be made based on your library's philosophy and in conjunction with other departments to ensure that the informational and educational needs of your community are being met.

Eleven percent of public libraries do not have a young adult collection or section. Fifty-eight percent of public libraries provide a section for young adults—that is, they have a separate young adult room or area where the young adult collection is housed. Fifteen percent have a young adult collection of materials but it is shelved with the adult collection, and 16 percent of all public libraries shelve young adult materials in the children's section.[1]

Fiction

Teens, like adults, read fiction for many reasons. For some, it is a means of escaping the pressures of their daily lives; for others, it is a safe way to "experiment" with situations they may encounter in the future. For many YAs, fiction provides insights into people with belief systems different from theirs and provides real "food for thought" in developing their own unique perspective on the world.

Many YAs prefer paperbacks to hardcover books because they are lighter, travel more easily, and are less conspicuous (particularly significant for teens self-conscious about their reading interests in the presence of peers who can be very judgmental). However, often the newest YA titles are published in hardcover only, and many teens would gladly read the hardcover of their favorite author's latest book rather than wait for it to come out in paperback. Hardcovers obviously hold up to multiple uses better than paperbacks, although paperbacks are cheaper to replace. As a general rule, a young adult collection should emphasize paperback titles, but not to the exclusion of hardcovers.

Series

Younger adolescents often go through a stage in which they read only series books such as *Sweet Valley High* and *Fear Street*. Although adults are eager to encourage these students to diversify their reading, the series genre may meet some normal adolescent developmental needs for control and predictability. In a time of life when their bodies and emotions are rapidly changing, many young teens take comfort in the familiar characters and predictable plots of series novels.

Realistic Fiction

Realistic fiction is often popular with young adults because it reflects their everyday reality, which is so often overlooked or misrepresented in popular culture. Realistic teen fiction deals with issues such as school, sports, religion, alcohol and drug abuse, friendships and betrayals, first sexual experiences, sexual orientation, violence and murder, which many teens encounter in the course of growing up. Reading about these issues in story form often encourages teens to consider how they would react in similar circumstances, which helps them develop into responsible adults. YA realistic fiction is often written from the first-person perspective of a teen narrator in accessible language, which also helps the teen reader to more readily identify with the characters and situations presented.

Genre Fiction

Like adults, many teens are drawn to genre fiction. Mystery and horror are genres that have particular appeal with many YAs, as evidenced by the popularity of such YA authors as R. L. Stine, Christopher Pike, and Lois Duncan, and adult authors such as Stephen King, Mary Higgins Clark, and Dean Koontz. Teens who read science fiction and fantasy tend to read voraciously, thereby justifying a good representation of this genre in your collection. Other popular genres with YAs include romance, Christian fiction, historical fiction, and adventure and outdoor fiction.

Popular Topics for YA Nonfiction

AIDS
autobiography
biography
sex
fashion
drugs and alcohol
college and career information
hobbies
humor
games
graphic novels
cartooning
music
sports
occult

Nonfiction

Young adults read nonfiction for two reasons: because they want to and because they have to.

Popular Nonfiction

The books that they want to read are those we will refer to as popular interest materials. These books address issues and concerns that teens are dealing with and need more information about, or, more commonly, focus on their recreational interests and hobbies. Personal interest materials often have a high impulse component as well—good cover art or a "hot topic" will cause teens to pick up these books.

Reluctant readers often prefer nonfiction books because they appeal to outside interests (which may not include reading), they often have photos and sparse text, and they can be browsed rather than read from cover to cover. YALSA's annual list of "Quick Picks for Reluctant Young Adult Readers" includes many popular nonfiction titles.

Some teens are only interested in reading "true" stories, ranging from biographies and autobiographies of favorite movie, sports, and music celebrities to stories of survival or of overcoming seemingly insurmountable odds. Diary-style accounts of teens encountering issues such as pregnancy, drug abuse, and suicide are also popular. The appeal of such stories lies in name recognition or in the sheer emotional drama of what the people endure. The people in the stories do not necessarily need to be teenagers themselves, although stories from an adolescent perspective often have added appeal.

A genre of popular nonfiction that is often overlooked is humor. Jokes, riddles, and humorous commentary are tremendously popular with teens, possibly because they provide a respite from many of the serious issues that they deal with in their everyday lives, and also because we all love to laugh.

Curricular Nonfiction

Nonfiction books that YAs have to read are those that support the curriculum. If your YA department provides homework support, it will need to contain materials to support the most common assignments given by teachers at your local schools. There are many nonfiction series designed to address issues that are frequently targeted in assignments. Resources such as *SIRS* and *Facts on File,* as well as many CD-ROM and online resources, may also be useful in assisting YAs in finding information for assignments. Many libraries also offer *Cliff's Notes,* which are frequently in demand with teens.

Magazines

The brief length of articles, pertinent topics, and glossy eye-catching layout of magazines have great YA appeal. Many libraries choose to place the YA magazine display in a prominent location to lure teens into the YA area. Some degree of damage and theft are inevitable with this medium, as the pages and binding are not made to withstand multiple uses. But the popularity of magazines with YAs more than makes up for the wear and tear on your collection. If you are unsure about what titles are popular with the teens in your area, ask local bookstore owners what magazines teens are buying or bring your Teen Advisory Board to select some sample titles themselves. The same collection development criteria that you use for your book collection should apply to the purchase of YA magazines.

Comic Books and Graphic Novels

Comic books and graphic novels (comics in book form) are an excellent addition to your YA collection because they appeal to teens who are more visually oriented and can even assist teens who have difficulty reading. Although many of the old favorites such as *Archie, Batman, Superman,* and *Wonder Woman* still enjoy teen appeal, newer comics such as *X-Men* and graphic novels that tackle real-life issues such as the Holocaust and incest are gaining in popularity. The topics and levels of sophistication vary widely between titles and warrant careful selection. The owners of comic book stores are often very knowledgeable about what titles are popular with teens in your area and may be willing to assist you in selecting titles to meet your library's selection criteria. Many comic books can be put on standing order through jobbers, and they can also be cataloged and prepared for circulation in the same way as magazines.

Computers

With ever-increasing amounts of information becoming available in electronic formats, technology holds a very important place in the young adult collection. Although the number of schools with Internet access had increased to 65 percent in 1996, only about 24 percent of classrooms had access to the Internet at that time.[2] According to a *Newsweek* poll conducted in 1997, "teens from families earning less than $25,000 a year were twice as likely to say they never use a computer at home."[3] As teachers and employers increasingly expect junior high and high school students to be computer literate, the public library may be the only resource for teens from lower-income families to conduct electronic research outside of school.

An MCI study released April 15, 1998, indicated that "the number of public libraries offering public access to the Internet has more than doubled the last two years to 60 percent."[4] Many of these libraries have

---

89% of teens use computers at least several times per week.

61% surf the Internet.

Boys edge out girls in online experience (66 to 56%).

Wealthier kids are more likely to have surfed.

92% think computers will improve their educational opportunities.

98% credit technology for making a positive difference in their lives.[5]

Users have the right to be free of unreasonable limitations or conditions set by libraries, librarians, system administrators, vendors, network service providers, or others.

The rights of users who are minors shall in no way be abridged.

Electronic information, services, and networks provided directly or indirectly by the library should be equally, readily, and equitably accessible to all library users.[6]

According to a 1998 survey:

73% of U.S. public libraries (over 15,700 central libraries and branches) offer public Internet access.

84% of the libraries in urban areas offer Internet access.

77% of the libraries in suburban areas offer Internet access.

68% of the libraries in rural areas offer Internet access.

74% of libraries with public Internet access have three or fewer workstations.

15% of libraries with public Internet access use filters on some or all of their workstations.

85% of public libraries with Internet access have an acceptable-use policy in place.[7]

found that offering access to electronic resources is a great way to draw more teens into the library.

As with books, YAs use CD-ROM and online resources because they want to and because they have to. Frequently, the resources that they want to use include e-mail, chat rooms, and games. Resources that they have to use include word processing, scholarly databases, college and job search banks, online newspapers, and subject-specific databases and Web sites.

Libraries that establish Internet use policies should take both the educational and recreational needs of teens into consideration. Through e-mail and chat rooms, teens may establish friendships and exchange information with peers around the world. Frequently, electronic games encourage creative thought and problem-solving skills. It is not the responsibility of the librarian to monitor patrons' use of electronic resources, nor to pass judgment on how patrons choose to use the resources that are made available to them, provided their behavior is not disruptive to others. However, you will want to provide some online safety guidelines. For a sample, see "Basic Rules of Online Safety for Teens" on page 110.

Some libraries have established time limits on the use of electronic resources in order to provide more equitable access to all patrons. Such policies should be enforced equitably, regardless of the age of the patron or the purpose for which she or he is using the resource.

One component of your YA collection may be a young adult page on your library's Web site. This page should provide information about young adult services in your library as well as links to sites that are of interest to teens. Many libraries have also incorporated reviews of books, movies, Web sites, and so on, and recommended reading lists, as well as more interactive services such as online writing contests or summer reading activities. Involve your Teen

Advisory Board in the creation of your library's YA page to ensure that the site will have real teen appeal.

Promoting Access to the Internet

Educate yourself, your staff, library board, governing bodies, community leaders, parents, and elected officials about the Internet and how best to take advantage of the wealth of information available. For examples of what other libraries have done, contact the ALA Public Information Office at 800-545-2433, ext. 5044 or http://www.ala.org/pio/

Uphold the First Amendment by establishing and implementing written guidelines and policies on Internet use in your library in keeping with your library's overall policies on access to library materials. For information about and copies of the Library Bill of Rights and its Interpretation of Electronic Information, Services and Networks, contact the ALA Office for Intellectual Freedom at 800-545-2433, ext. 4223 or oif@ala.org

The ALA Office for Intellectual Freedom has published a "Statement on Library Use of Filtering Software" that includes the following answers to "What Can Your Library Do to Promote Access to the Internet?"

Promote Internet use by facilitating user access to Web sites that satisfy user interest and needs.

Create and promote library Web pages designed both for general use and for use by children. These pages should point to sites that have been reviewed by library staff.

Consider using privacy screens or arranging terminals away from public view to protect a user's confidentiality.

Provide information and training for parents and minors that remind users of time, place and manner restrictions on Internet use.

Establish and implement user behavior policies.[8]

AV Materials

Today's YAs are the first generation to have grown up watching videos and listening to music and books on compact disc. Multimedia is a way of life for them, and they expect to be able to

The people who started college in 1998 were born in 1980.

Atari predates them, as do vinyl albums.

The expression "you sound like a broken record" means nothing to them.

They may have heard of eight-track, but chances are they probably have never actually seen or heard one.

The digital disc was introduced when they were one year old.

They have always had answering machines.

Most have never seen a TV set with only thirteen channels.

They were born the year that Walkman was introduced by Sony.

Current YALSA book lists can be found on the YALSA Web site: http://www.ala.org/yalsa. They can also be ordered through fax-on-demand: 800-545-2433 (press 8). ALA's *Guide to Best Reading* can be ordered by phone: 800-545-2433 (press 7) or fax: 312-836-9958.

access information in various formats at their school and public libraries. Regardless of whether your library has a separate audiovisual collection, consider adding AV materials to your young adult collection. Books on tape and CD can be interfiled with your YA fiction and nonfiction. Videos can be paired with books to increase the appeal of both formats. AV displays can be used to lure otherwise reluctant teens into your YA area.

Collection Development

Determining what specific materials young adults want and need can sometimes be challenging, but there are many resources available to help guide your decisions. In addition to the standard review sources discussed later in this chapter, don't forget to use your own skills of observation to tailor your collection to the interests of teens in your community. See the Appendixes, pages 111–114, for sample guidelines for assessing nonfiction, literature, and Web sites for young adults.

The middle school and high school curricula should guide your selections for materials that will be used primarily for homework support. Many nonfiction series exist primarily to address issues that are frequently assigned by middle school and high school teachers. These series include Opposing Viewpoints (Greenhaven), Encyclopedia of Health (Chelsea House), Impact Books (Watts) and Everything You Need to Know (Rosen), among others.

Personal interests can be gleaned from many secondary sources such as teen magazines; texts on adolescent development; other adults who work with adolescents in the community; and colleagues, teachers, and parents. There is no substitute, however, for asking the kids themselves, either formally or informally. Never ask "What can the library do for you?" because most young adults cannot answer and the question itself implies more choices to the young adult than the library may be able to deliver. Ask instead about favorite hobbies, magazines, musicians, television shows, movies, and sports. If you have teenagers of your own, observe where they hang out, what they like to do for recreation, and what kinds of things they buy, and use this information to drive your selection decisions for your YA collection.

Three journals publish reviews and articles primarily of interest to young adult librarians:

ALAN Review (ISSN 0882-2840)
National Council of Teachers of English
1111 Kenyon Road
Urbana, IL 61801-1096

Kliatt (ISSN 1065-8602)
33 Bay State Road
Wellesley, MA 02181-3244

Voice of Youth Advocates (ISSN 0160-4201)
4720A Boston Way
Lanham, MD 20706

Many other journals such as *Booklist, Bulletin for the Center of Children's Books, Horn Book, Journal of Youth Services in Libraries*, and *School Library Journal* also address YA issues, although their scope is broader.

There are also annual lists of new and recommended resources produced by several of the above journals as well as by YALSA and various libraries. Retrospective lists are also published in monograph form at regular intervals. For bibliographic information, contact http://www.ala.org/yalsa/professional/yasrvcsbib.html

Before using any of these tools, it is important to think about several things. First, decide which topics seem to be of broad interest and concentrate on them before branching out into lesser interests. Second, think about formats.

Since more and more teens are using the Internet, it is important to consider the selection of Web sites for YAs as well as more traditional library materials. YALSA has created an Internet guide for teens called Teen Hoopla (www.ala.org/teenhoopla), which is an excellent starting point to find appropriate links for the YA page of your library's Web site. *Voice of Youth Advocates* (VOYA) has also instituted a column called "YA Clicks," which reviews Web sites of interest to young adults and their librarians.

... the high school section has dramatically improved in terms of quality, etc. Less emphasis is placed on series books like *Sweet Valley High,* etc., and more now on actual substantial literature (like comics ... joke). Really, though, if you'd told me a few years ago there were books on art and philosophy in the high school section, I woulda (sic) just laughed. I think that the existence of and participation in the Council has made me more aware of that section. Going to book buying outings allows me to have some control as to what goes in there. I think having real teenagers pick out the contents has changed it into a formidable part of the library. Real high school students go in there now, not just the bookish ones or junior high girls.[9]

Many selection tools that identify resources of interest to young adults emphasize books over other media. Although several journals now review AV materials, CD-ROMs, and even Web sites, you may need to be more creative in identifying ways to determine what titles in these formats are popular with teens. Visit local video stores, comic book stores, and newsstands, and take your Teen Advisory Board with you. Watch television shows identified by young adults themselves or by critics as having high teen appeal. This will help you recommend and display materials in your library's collection that would otherwise be overlooked, as well as allow you to purchase materials and provide links from your library's Web site that better represent young adult interests, or to make suggestions for such purchases to the staff responsible for collection development.

NOTES

1. U.S. Department of Education, Office of Educational Research and Improvement, National Center for Education Statistics, *Services and Resources for Children and Young Adults in Public Libraries* (Washington, D.C.: U.S. Government Printing Office, 1995), 37.

2. U.S. Department of Education, National Center for Education Statistics, *Library Statistics of Colleges and Universities,* various years; and Integrated Postsecondary Education Data System, "Academic Library Survey."

3. "Teenagers and Technology," *Newsweek,* April 28, 1997, p. 86.

4. "MCI Study Shows Internet Use at Libraries on the Rise," *ALA News Release* 3, no. 19, April 1998.

5. "Teenagers and Technology," p. 86.

6. American Library Association, Office for Intellectual Freedom, "Access to Electronic Information, Services and Networks: An Interpretation of the Library Bill of Rights," adopted by the ALA Council, January 24, 1996.

7. "ALA News," *American Libraries,* October 1998, p. 6.

8. From American Library Association, Intellectual Freedom Committee, "Statement on Library Use of Filtering Software," July 1, 1997.

9. Michael Quilligan, member of the Carmel Clay (Ind.) Public Library Teen Library Council, 1998, on how council involvement has affected the library's services to young adults.

6

Serving Young Adults

Marketing and Publicity

In 1998, American teenagers were estimated to spend $119 billion.[1] With this kind of spending power, marketers have taken note of what appeals to teens. Librarians don't need to reinvent the wheel. We can learn a tremendous amount by observing the strategies of retailers in creating advertising and displays that target young adults.

Lack of knowledge about library services is a factor in choosing not to use the public library for 70 percent of young adults.[2] "Marketers know that if they attract someone as a teen, there's a good chance they'll keep him or her as a customer in the years ahead."[3] They also know that teen opinions influence the behaviors of their friends and families. Turning a teen on to the library may also encourage library use by their classmates, siblings, and parents.

"To lure teen customers, many companies are practicing 'relationship marketing'."[4] They are inviting teen input through interactive Web sites, online bulletin boards, newsletters, and teen consulting groups in order to keep their finger on the pulse of the ever-changing trends in the lives of young adults. Librarians have a lot to gain from emulating these marketers. By not talking down to teens in their advertising, marketers also hope to appeal to adults who come across ads that are targeted at teens. "Neutrogena Corp., for example, strives to talk to teens in the same language and images it uses with adults."[5] Targeting more sophisticated ads at teens also avoids alienating young adults by stereotyping them as children.

One of the most powerful tools we can borrow from the extensive experience of retail stores is merchandising. The power of merchandising comes from principles of human engineering. People look for ways to focus the eye when presented with a vast array of visual stimuli. People also follow predictable traffic patterns. Merchandising uses this knowledge to set up displays to focus the eye within prime traffic areas. In libraries, these areas are

1. The front of the building (i.e., the first twenty feet of space)
2. The ends of aisles
3. The point of circulation (on top of, en route to, and down the sides of the circulation desk)
4. High traffic, open spaces

Special paperback displays called "dumps" can be strategically placed in these spaces. The space itself will do the work for you. A casual study of a shopping mall or book, music, or video store will give you a good visual idea of ways to merchandise materials. Some public libraries have used video store display fixtures successfully to merchandise library materials. These are the places to load up with high-interest materials. While nobody visits every single aisle of the library stacks, nearly everyone walks past the ends of aisles to get to a specific spot. The ends of stacks make great display spots for popular young adult materials. Another place of high visibility is near the checkout desk, either on the desk itself or on tables near where people stand in line to check out at peak periods.

Besides placing the right materials in the right formats in the right spots, it is important to remember to display them face out (with the front of the cover showing) for maximum visual appeal, just as video stores do. This kind of display technique is designed to attract browsers' attention (see figure 6.1). Since many young adults loathe the idea of asking adults for help, the use of self-help browsing merchandising techniques is an unobtrusive and attractive means of serving them. These space utilization and display techniques are often so successful that staff have trouble keeping the display spaces filled. There is also the occasional problem of someone seeking a specific item that is on display. If your library has the capability of changing the

FIGURE 6.1 █ **Merchandising Works—Display Ideas**

Super Sport

> Biographies of athletes, sports card collecting, *Sports Illustrated,* series *(Hoops, Blitz, Dojo Rats)*, techniques (skiing, in-line skating, skateboarding, soccer, wrestling), sports genre titles

Humor Hotline

> Comics, cartoon series (*Garfield, Calvin & Hobbes, Far Side, Cathy,* Matt Groenig's *Life Is Hell* series), joke books, trivia, *Ripley's Believe It or Not,* humor genre lists

Chillers and Thrillers

> Pike, Stine, mystery series by authors such as Lois Duncan, Joan Lowry Nixon, Jay Bennett, classics *(Frankenstein, Dracula, Dr. Jekyll and Mr. Hyde)*, thrillers and horror series, horror genre titles, "true" ghost stories

How-to Helpers

> Video game tips, crafts, cartooning and drawing, hair styles and makeup, bodybuilding, astrology, hobbies, babysitting

Issues and Answers

> Jobs, careers, substance abuse, teen pregnancy and sexuality, social and developmental issues (school, peer pressure, family problems)

SOURCE: Adapted from Mary Arnold, "Merchandising Works" (A handout from Serving the Underserved II, a seminar conducted by the Young Adult Library Services Association of the American Library Association, January 1996, in San Antonio, Texas), 3-18.

status of items in the catalog to show that they are in a temporary display, this can eliminate some confusion. If not, having a few items out of classification order is a small price to pay for higher circulation to teenagers. While such merchandising is impersonal in terms of interaction with young adult patrons, it is a powerful and dynamic method for moving materials. Keeping the displays well stocked is a high priority.

A more personal type of collection promotion is to set up ways in which teens can promote materials directly to their peers. Some libraries have encouraged teens to create book covers for books with YA appeal but unattractive cover art. You could also put short review forms or reader's annotations for young adult readers in materials as they circulate, or ask for nominations for "Books I Would Like All My Friends (or Parents or Teachers) to Read!" and publish or display the results.

The Carmel Clay (Ind.) Public Library has instituted a permanent "Choice Picks" collection of titles that have received the votes of three or more Teen Library Council members.

Bibliographies or bookmarks with lists of recommended titles can also be useful marketing tools. It's better to hand them to young adults or distribute them in the classroom than to simply put them out on a table or shelf, however. Pithy, clever annotations can also increase the appeal of titles on a list. For "How to Write a Reader's Annotation," see page 115.

Lists and displays also need to be coordinated with relevant programs both inside and outside the library, whether library sponsored or not. Remember that the young adults themselves can help generate display ideas and posters.

How to use book lists effectively:

- force feed—put a copy into items borrowed by YAs
- place lists, with a large sign, inside the entrance to the YA area
- distribute lists to patrons who ask relevant reader's advisory questions[6]

Reader's Advisory

Questions to Ask in a Reader's Advisory Encounter

1. Are you looking for any particular type of book?

2. What books or authors have you enjoyed reading?

3. Are you looking for something to read for fun or for an assignment? Often books read for assignments have to meet certain criteria, such as length, genre, historical period, and so on.

4. After recommending several titles: Is this the type of thing that you are looking for?

It is always a good idea to recommend several titles and to ask patrons to let you know what they thought of them afterward.

Reader's Advisory can be one of the most fun and rewarding aspects of young adult librarianship. Many librarians go into the field because of their love for books and reading, and reader's advisory offers us the opportunity to share our love of literature by helping teens find books that meet their needs and interests. The time and effort that you spend poring over journals and teen magazines, observing popular culture, and interacting with teens, all as part of collection development, will serve you well when it comes time to match your young patrons with appropriate materials in your collection.

A familiarity with your young adult collection (and with materials in the juvenile and adult collections that are appropriate for YAs) is essential to be able to provide good reader's advisory service. Librarians must push themselves beyond the boundaries of personal interest to become familiar with titles from a wide variety of genres to meet the needs of the ninth grade boy who reads only horror and real-life adventure stories as well as the sixth grade girl looking for Christian romance and the high school student who has just discovered Ayn Rand.

Start by reading, viewing, and listening to the materials in your collection. You don't have to know every word or frame of every item, just enough to get a good idea of what happens. Reading time can often be scarce in a busy library. Many librarians choose to take materials from their collection home to read in their free time. Although this is often unavoidable for those determined to have a thorough knowledge of their collection, reading young adult materials is necessary in order to provide good service to your teen patrons and should not be looked upon as "wasting time" at work. Take advantage of snatches of time such as lags between serving patrons at a public service desk or the moments when colleagues are gathering to begin a meeting to browse through new YA materials before they go out on the shelf. When time permits, balance the obligation of becoming familiar with the materials in your collection with your other job-related tasks. Your patrons and colleagues will benefit from your familiarity with YA authors and your ability to knowledgeably discuss the issues presented in their books.

In thinking about how you would describe a title to young adults, practice using adjectives that make the book sound interesting, exciting, or fun. Avoid getting bogged down in every detail of the plot; instead, try to give the patron a "feel" for the book with a few pithy sentences. Don't gloss over serious or controversial issues, however. Patrons deserve to know what major themes they may encounter in a novel and to decide for themselves whether they choose to read about such topics. Try out your "spiels" on family and friends and then on teenagers themselves. These spiels are technically called "short booktalks," "jacket talks," or "shelf talks." Basically, they are like television commercials—thirty seconds of verbal promotion for a particular title.

More formal, lengthy, or elaborate booktalks can be used in classroom settings or to present a variety of titles to a group of students who are visiting the library. For "How to Write Your Own Booktalk," and for "Tips on Booktalking to a Group," see pages 117 and 118.

To help you keep track of the young adult titles you read, consider creating a reading log. As soon as possible after reading, viewing, or listening to an item in your collection, jot down a few notes about the content. Index cards, three-ring binders, or computer databases may all be used to organize these notes. Consider including some or all of the following information, based on how you intend to use your reading log:

title, author, date of publication, photocopy of cover art

intended audience or appropriate audience, in your opinion

written booktalk, highlighting the strengths of the work to entice others to read it

brief plot summary, including names of main characters to refresh your memory

your opinion, to spark your memory when discussing the work informally with others

possible objections, to tailor your recommendation to an appropriate audience or to inform a patron with particular sensibilities about controversial topics

page numbers of paragraphs to read aloud

citations of reviews

related works—other titles that might appeal to someone who liked this book

Your reading log may be used to create more formal booktalks for group presentations or to spark your memory in providing an individual reader's advisory. Keeping track of what you have read will also help you direct your reading so you do not inadvertently avoid topics and authors that may appeal more to young adults than to you. Regardless of how you do it, some sort of reading log usually helps in remembering a title once you have finished it. Sometimes staff units keep a multiple reader log or notebook handy so that everybody using a service desk can benefit from communal reading, viewing, and listening knowledge. Sharing titles at staff meetings also helps keep up with new or previously unknown titles.

One of YALSA's electronic discussion lists, YALSA-BK, is a vibrant forum for discussing all aspects of young adult literature, and it will be particularly helpful for the librarian who is the only person in her or his library designated to serve YAs. To subscribe, send a message to listproc@ala.ala.org. Include the "subscribe" command in the body of the message, as follows:

subscribe YALSA-BK

When assisting young adults with reader's advisory questions, it is helpful to use an abbreviated form of the reference interview in order to determine what type of material the patron enjoys reading and what he or she is looking for in this particular visit to the library. Patrons with reader's advisory questions may or may not approach the librarian for a recommendation. Many teens do not realize that some librarians read young adult literature, and they are often pleasantly surprised to find an adult who is knowledgeable about their favorite authors and titles.

Often parents approach the librarian, looking for titles to recommend to their teenage children. If the YA is present, try to address him or her directly to find out his or her individual interests, rather than relying on the perception of the parent. Sometimes, the parent has concerns about issues such as language, violence, or explicit sexual content. It is important to honor these concerns and help find materials that meet the parent's criteria and still appeal to his or her child's interests. If the YA returns unaccompanied by his or her parent, it is not the librarian's responsibility to enforce the restrictions that the parent had expressed earlier. The librarian should instead conduct a reader's advisory interview with the YA to determine his or her individual needs and interests.

Following up on reader's advisory recommendations the next time you see a YA patron is an excellent way to establish a rapport based on books with your regular patrons. Most teens will be impressed if you remember their reading interests from one visit to the next. They will often be willing to discuss their opinions about the books you've recommended and even suggest other titles that you may not be familiar with. These encounters with teens about books will not only help you stay abreast of YA interests, but will often provide the deep satisfaction of knowing that your interaction with teen patrons has resulted in mutual enjoyment, learning, and growth.

Reference and Homework Support

Many young adults, including those who might not use the library for any other reason, do use it when they need information and help to complete their homework assignments.

The homework support experience gives you the opportunity to interact directly with a sizable segment of your library users. In addition to satisfying teenagers' informational needs, you can help them develop a positive attitude toward reference services. Youth advocates are fond of pointing out that it gives you an opportunity for public relations and a chance to shape positive attitudes toward the library among tomorrow's taxpayers and voters. This is certainly something to remember, but primarily you should help them because they are your patrons today and they need your help today.

Whose Job Is It, Anyway?

It is important to consider a fundamental question at this point: Should the public library be concerned with homework support at all? Isn't that the place of the school library media center?

There are stories of public libraries with specific policies stating that they will not "help" students with homework questions, either through collection development ("We are not the school library") or through telephone reference services ("You have to come to the library for that"). It is interesting to note that many of these same libraries are so eager to "help" other segments of the community that they are more than willing to expend resources of time and money promoting services such as online searching and telephone reference to those groups.

Adults go to work for eight hours a day. Adolescents go to school for eight hours a day. Going to school could be called the "work" of young adults. While acknowledging that it cannot take the place of an in-house, "special" library, the public library is willing to support the work of local businesspersons and professionals through collection development, and it respects their reference questions. In the interest of equitable service, while the public library does not take the place of a school library media center, it has a responsibility to support the work of students, young and old, by developing collections to support their work and by treating their questions with respect.

Moreover, not all students may be able to use a school library media center: they may be home-schooled, their school may not have one, and even if one exists, after-school responsibilities (such as caring for younger siblings, extra-curricular activities, part-time jobs), busing, or shrinking school budgets that limit size and accessibility of the school library media center may make the public library the only agency available to many students seeking information for homework assignments. At best, you can collaborate with school library media centers to provide library services to young adults. At worst, you may have to go it alone.

Being Prepared

"I'm doing a report on helium and my teacher says I can't use an encyclopedia."

"I've got to find five books, three magazine articles, and three newspaper articles on Chaucer."

"My friend and I have got Mr. Impossible for sophomore English and we both need three novels by twentieth-century American writers. I need three that use stream of consciousness and she needs three that use flash-backs or foreshadowing."

Many of the problems encountered in providing home-work support to young adults can be avoided or at least greatly reduced if you're prepared. Far too often, you find yourself at a busy reference desk helping patron after patron when sud-denly you're confronted with the "Homework Assignment from Hell." It's far too current or too specialized for the library to have much more than a few periodical articles on it, thirty students needing three sources each for it will be requesting the same information over the course of the evening, *and* it's due tomorrow. It would be easier to cope with such a situation if you knew it was coming and if you had previously taken steps to deal with it. For this reason, you should try to improve communication with the schools and with your colleagues in the library. You can become proactive and take steps to pre-pare yourself.

Before offering suggestions for preparation, a few brief comments are in order. As busy as you are, the last thing you want is to make more work for yourself. To be sure, imple-menting any of the following suggestions will involve your time and energy. But this can be viewed as an investment; there will be a payoff, and your efforts will save you time and energy later. Also, you will not have time to implement all the suggestions. But each one you can implement will help you, your colleagues, and your young adult patrons.

Work with the Schools

While their objectives differ, both schools and public libraries are concerned with the education of the young adults they serve. It would seem logical for those individuals who are in the public library and those who are in the schools to communi-cate and cooperate in order to simplify their lives and to maxi-mize their powerful allies and helpful colleagues. Work with and through them whenever possible in your dealings with a school. Work with media specialists to involve teachers in pro-viding homework information. Share assignment information with each other. When working with individual teachers, show your respect for the school library media specialist's territory by keeping that person informed of your communications and activities. If you're unfamiliar with school library media centers, read *Information Power: Building Partnerships for Learning* for a general overview of the mission, goals, activities, and responsibilities of school library media staff members and programs.[7] It includes *Information Literacy Standards for Student Learning* (also available as a separate publication) that public librarians can use in their work with school-age patrons.[8] By becoming familiar with the staff and resources of local school library media centers, sharing information, and working with someone in the school, you can avoid duplication of effort and wasted time. If the school with which you are working has no school library media specialist, work with the principal or someone designated by the principal.

Getting information to and from school library media specialists and teachers can be difficult. Remember, they are usually overwhelmed with material to read, so don't plan on lengthy written communications. Furthermore, presentations at large faculty meetings may not be the most effective way of communicating information.

Planning

Obtaining copies of school daily schedules and yearly calendars can help you in your planning. If school library media specialists meet regularly at the district level, ask to meet with them or invite them to your staff meetings or hold a joint meeting. You can make arrangements to meet with small groups of teachers, by department or grade level, at the building or district level. One method is to invite school staff to open house at the public library for donuts early in the morning or refreshments at the end of their day or during an in-service day. You can also make appointments to meet or talk by phone with individual teachers during their lunch hours, their planning time, or after school. Short, eye-catching pieces in school district and public library newsletters disseminate information to and from school personnel. Brochures outlining the services you offer to teachers and their students can be distributed in teachers' mailboxes at the beginning of each school year. For one example of such a brochure, see "School Services at the Hinsdale Public Library" on page 120. Always remember to make arrangements through the appropriate channels.

In your communications with the schools, be positive and constructive, stating your desire to be of help to curriculum directors, school library media specialists, teachers, and students. Stress that the goal you all share is to help students succeed. Emphasize your concern that students' homework experiences in the public library be positive and productive, not frustrating and unprofitable.

School Assignments
and the Library

Whether you work with school library media specialists or independently, whenever and however you eventually communicate with individuals or groups of teachers, encourage them to think about their assignments. Suggest they ask themselves these basic questions: Does the assignment call for work in the public library, the school library, or both? Would it be more appropriate for students to consider alternative sources such as personal interviews for local history assignments or visits to a local academic library for use of journals or government documents?

Since most assignments probably involve use of the public library, teachers should also consider the purpose of each assignment. Is it primarily intended to teach the student how to use a library and its tools (the catalog, periodical indexes, the Internet)? Or is the acquisition or refinement of information literacy skills an ancillary part of the instructional activity? Does it really matter if the student finds articles through a periodical index or if the librarian supplies the student with either a bibliography of relevant articles or a printout of the articles themselves from a full-text database?

Ask teachers to consider whether a particular assignment as given to students is essentially an assignment for the librarian more than for the student. Too often, a student will come to the library and approach a very busy librarian with a difficult question but without clear (or clearly understood) instruction or suggestions from the teacher. If the librarian is to provide adequate guidance for students in this situation, a considerable expenditure of time, thought, and effort may be required. The librarian needs to decipher the question and then work with the student to access, both intellectually and physically, a source that will provide the information. Meanwhile, other patrons may be kept waiting. Such a situation can have negative consequences for all involved: the student may come away from the situation empty-handed, the teacher may be disappointed in the student's "failure," the librarian may be resentful of the teacher, the other patrons may grow impatient. Encourage teachers to consider how and where students might find the information when they pose a question, and to provide students with suggested avenues for finding an answer, as well as clear instructions for completing an assignment. Keep in mind, however, that some teachers, no matter how well-intentioned they may be, do not understand how to use libraries.

Teachers also need to think about prohibiting or requiring use of particular formats such as restricting use of encyclopedias or requiring use of the Internet for particular assignments. Remind them that frequently the most appropriate source for information may be a general or subject-specific encyclopedia or other resource in print rather than electronic format. Encourage them to direct their students to their preferred format as a starting point, and then, if possible, to find an additional source. Request that all teachers include the phrase "or anything else suggested by the librarian" on all assignments to give you adequate leeway when anticipated materials are unavailable.

Finally, ask them to think about the problems associated with, and the advisability of, "mass assignments." These assignments require large groups of students to read the same book or report on the same topic. While mass assignments may make life easier for the teacher, they frequently create massive frustration for the students and for both the school library media center and the public library. Such assignments usually result in the following scenario. The first few students to come to the library check out all the circulating books on the assigned subject, leaving their classmates with limited resources. Furthermore, reference materials may become damaged through heavy use or mutilated or stolen by desperate students. In addition, if large numbers of students have a short period of time in which to complete an assignment, there may be other problems such as a shortage of available search stations and microform readers or insufficient library space to accommodate all the students. Always remember to approach teachers with respect and courtesy. No matter how frustrated you may become with their assignments, emphasize your mutual goal of serving the students and focus on the benefits of cooperation.

Since you need to know what students will be looking for when they come to you, perhaps the most essential message to convey to the schools is that it is important for them to communicate with you about upcoming assignments while there is still time for feedback. This cannot be emphasized enough. Request copies of relevant documents, such as curriculum guides and textbooks, from the school. Curriculum guides can provide you with information about individual courses, including goals and objectives, activities, and resources recommended for use. Especially examine the district-level library or information skills curriculum guide, which can provide an overview of the integration of the entire scope and sequence of the instructional program. While working with students, you can instruct them or provide reinforcement of information literacy skills taught in their classes.

Early in the school year, ask school library media specialists and teachers to submit bibliographies of required and suggested titles as well as copies of assignments. Examine required reading lists and assignments and, keeping in mind the resources available at school, think about what's available in your library. Your collection development plan can address the deficiencies in your collection and designate areas for resource sharing. If you find that students will have difficulties completing an assignment given the combined resources of the school library media center and the public library, try to offer the teacher alternative resources. To encourage teachers to communicate with you throughout the school year, consider using "assignment alerts." These forms are particularly useful when printed as postage-paid self-mailers or postcards (see figure 6.2). The teachers only have to fill in the blanks and drop the completed forms in the mail. You can also send messages through e-mail, fax, or a dedicated phone line with an answering machine that is available at all hours for assignment-alert information. Or consider putting your assignment-alert form on the library's Web site and letting the school library media specialists and teachers know it's there so that they can transmit the forms back to the public library electronically.

If you receive an assignment alert form directly from a teacher, it is courteous to fax back the information to that teacher's media specialist, in case she or he is not yet aware of the assignment. It is also sometimes helpful to send out postcards or printed Post-its reminding teachers to use assignment-alert forms midway through each semester. Opening and maintaining these lines of communication between the schools and public libraries provide more opportunities for cooperation in offering homework support.

Sharing Resources

If student homework experiences in the public library are to be productive and positive, school library media specialists, teachers, and public librarians must communicate and share resources so each is familiar with the services and materials of

FIGURE 6.2 ▌ **Assignment Alert**

FAX or send ten days before start of assignment.
[Insert FAX and other address information.]

Teacher's Name _____

School Library Media Specialist's Name _____

School _____

Grade _____   Phone Number _____

Fax Number _____

Brief description of assignment / project (Please attach student's copy of assignment, if
available.)

_____

_____

_____

_____

Number of students working on this assignment _____

Assignment begins _____   ends _____

School media specialist has been notified of this assignment _____

With proper notification, our staff can:

    compile collections of the materials available for topics that are narrow or have limited
      resources

    provide call numbers of reference and circulating materials available for broad topics

    inform you via fax of the location and availability of materials in the public library

the others. When communicating with teachers, describe your
library's policies and procedures that might have an impact on
providing homework support services for students: hours
when the library is open, policies concerning telephone reference services, programs the library might offer on library use
instruction, availability of "pathfinders" or customized bibliographies, opportunities for patrons to check out reference
works or periodicals overnight, online searching services, interlibrary loan procedures, acquisition policies, and so on. You
can also collaborate with the schools to implement the *Information Literacy Standards for Student Learning.*[9] See page 124.

You can invite teachers and school library media specialists individually or in groups to the public library for a brief tour to familiarize themselves with your resources. Draw particular attention to the reference collection. Teachers might not be aware of some especially helpful reference works about which they could inform students, and school library media specialists will see how your collection complements theirs. Visit school library media centers to become familiar with their resources. Ask teachers to bring copies of their assignments with them. Collaborate with the school library media specialists to encourage the teachers to think about their students' chances for successfully completing their assignments and becoming information literate, given the resources that are readily available in the school library media center and the public library.

Keeping teachers informed of what the library can offer their students is an ongoing process and cannot be accomplished in a single contact. You need to evaluate assignments continually and, whenever problems arise, inform school library media specialists and teachers and discuss alternatives. The most direct way to do this is to call the school library media specialist (if there is one) and possibly individual teachers to discuss the assignment. However, since school library media specialists and teachers are frequently unavailable to answer phone calls, your time is limited, and the student is frequently quite anxious about having something to "hand in," an expeditious way of communicating problems with an assignment is the use of a notification form (see figure 6.3). You could include an adapted version of this form on your library's Web site as well.

Since the purpose of this form is to bring a problem to the attention of the school library media specialist and the teacher, it is important for it to begin with a positive statement such as "We welcome student use of the public library." The notification form should list frequently occurring problems such as all materials on the subject are on loan and not available; not enough materials are available to satisfy the number of students; the particular topic is too new or too specialized for there to be sufficient available materials; the assignment as written is unclear; or there are too many restrictions on the subject. This form can be copied for the student to present to the teacher, and a copy can be sent to the school library media specialist.

If the form is to be helpful, it should also include sufficient space to refer to specific problems and to suggest specific solutions. If it becomes apparent that the same problems may

FIGURE 6.3 █ *Parent/Teacher Notification Form*

Library: _____ Date: _____

Dear Parent/Teacher:

We welcome student use of the public library for personal enrichment or to supplement the school library media center's holdings for homework assignments. We work with the school library media specialists and teachers to implement the Standards for Student Learning that will result in information-literate graduates. Occasionally, however, certain situations restrict our ability to help. For example, when _____ came to the library today, we were unable to fill the request for _____ because:

1. _____ All material on the subject was already in use.
2. _____ Reasonable searches failed to supply suitable material.
3. _____ The types of materials the student could use were severely restricted.
4. _____ The best sources for the topic must be used in the library.
5. _____ Further clarification on the question is needed. Please call us.
6. _____ We are unable to provide the same material to so many students at one time.
7. _____ Material on the topic is also in demand by other library patrons.
8. _____ The assignment deadline does not allow time for interlibrary loan.
9. _____ Other: _____

_____

Please consider giving us advance notice of assignments so that we may better serve you.

Librarian: _____ Phone: _____

affect several students' successful completion of an assignment, note the specific problem(s) and solution(s) on one form and make several copies for easy distribution. In addition to improving communications with the schools, such notification forms provide an opportunity for good public relations. They show the students, their parents, and their teachers that you tried to help and that you are interested in finding ways to be of service.

Work within the Library

In a perfect world, all school library media specialists and teachers would unfailingly contact you in advance about upcoming assignments. Even in the real, less-than-perfect world, you will hear from some school library media specialists and teachers—particularly if you persist with follow-up contacts. But don't expect to hear from them all for every assignment.

Whenever a student approaches you with a reference question that appears to be a homework assignment, first determine whether it is indeed an assignment. This can be tricky in the case of questions about subjects of a personal nature (abortion, divorce, drug abuse, suicide, and so on). You may prefer to ask questions that narrow down the type of information the patron is seeking rather than the purpose for which she or he wants it. "Are you looking for research information, such as statistics on drug abuse in America, or more specific instructions on how an individual might overcome drug abuse?" rather than "Are you doing a school report on drug abuse or are you looking for self-help books?") Frequently, the student will specifically state that she or he is looking for information for an assignment. In that case, ask if the student has a handout from the teacher. If so, ask if you may make photocopies. Keeping photocopies of assignments available in a notebook for all staff to refer to can help you meet the immediate demands of students as well as plan for future assignments.

If there is no handout, ask some critical questions:

When is the assignment due?

Are there many students working on the same topic or do students have different topics?

How much information do you need?

Do you have to tell your teacher how and where you got the information (i.e., is the assignment designed to test information skills) or do you just need a simple answer?

Write a brief description of the assignment based on the response and note whatever sources were particularly helpful for this assignment. If possible, contact the school library media specialist or teacher to confirm the answers you received from the student and to get additional information. If you receive additional or revised information, you may need to amend your original description.

Once you have information about a homework assignment, don't keep it to yourself. Inform your library colleagues as soon as possible through the best available channel of communication—a department meeting, in person, or a note at the reference desk.

In addition to making copies of any homework handouts from students, make copies of descriptions you write or material from teachers and school library media specialists. File one of these copies as a master and keep another in a folder or notebook at the reference desk. You can direct other librarians to this source when you inform them about a current assignment. Also ask them to contribute information about assignments they discover. That way, all desk staff will have a single source of information about current homework assignments.

One of the more traditional methods of dealing with group assignments is to create a temporary reference shelf. This shelf may consist of only a few items: reference books that aren't encyclopedias, copies of a few important periodical articles, even one or two key books from the circulating collection. You may need to limit the time each student can use these high-demand items and also hold some form of identification to ensure their return to the reserve shelf. If more than one department is serving students with the same assignment (i.e., Children's and Reference), develop a system for sharing assignment information between departments so that students are referred to the most appropriate place for resources. Reserve shelves maximize access to key sources of information for all students working on an assignment and minimalize theft and mutilation of materials.

There are other tools for dealing with group assignments. "Pathfinders" can help students and other patrons find their way to information on a subject by providing relevant subject headings and indexing terms used in encyclopedias, periodical indexes, the vertical file, the library catalog, and electronic resources. You can also include names of individuals associated with the subject (authors who have written in the field, key figures about whom there may be biographical information, and so on) or a list of call numbers for materials with relevant information. While "pathfinders" won't solve the problem caused when the few early birds get all the circulating "worms," they will greatly reduce the time spent in repeatedly providing the same directions to large numbers of students as well as suggesting sources that the student might not have considered. See "Pathfinder" on page 122 for one example.

Customized bibliographies on assigned topics that reflect library holdings can also be created. This is a good way to avoid the frustration that results when students come in with reading lists containing titles that you don't own. These bibliographies are especially helpful when there isn't enough time to order materials through interlibrary loan.

If at all possible, create pathfinders and bibliographies in conjunction with the appropriate school library media specialist. By including information that reflects the collections at both the public library and the school library media center, you can do much to increase students' chances of finding useful material. At the same time, you are promoting a holistic view of libraries. Young adults may begin to see how different types of libraries are connected and to gain an appreciation of libraries as a networked community of information resources that are willing to work together to meet their patrons' needs.

Another way to provide homework support in the public library is through the establishment and availability of "homework help centers" at various times during the school year, particularly when requests for help with term paper research are heaviest. These centers can be staffed by volunteers—currently employed or retired teachers, parents, or even older students. With minimal "refresher" training in library use and a basic introduction to the techniques of the reference interview, the use of volunteer homework helpers can be a viable alternative, particularly in understaffed and overworked situations. While setting up homework help centers could require a major investment of time and resources, there is no reason not to initiate a discussion about their feasibility. Volunteers who serve as tutors or homework helpers are no less valuable than literacy volunteers. As of August 1995, homework assistance programs were available to young adults in only 12 percent of public libraries.[10]

Another way of providing homework assistance to your patrons is to create a homework help site on your library's home page that bookmarks subject-specific sites and research tools on the Internet. Homework support Web sites were reviewed in the "YA Clicks" column of VOYA, v. 21, no. 2, June 1998 in an article called "Help for the Homeworkers" by Patrick Jones, Renée Vaillancourt, and the Carmel Clay (Ind.) Public Library Teen Library Council. You can also find links to sites that are useful for homework support on the Young Adult Librarian's Help/Home Page (http://yahelp.suffolk.lib.ny.us) and TeenHoopla (http://www.ala.org/teenhoopla).

While preparing to provide homework support to young adults or working with them, you may notice areas of your collection that need to be improved. Once again, communicate with your colleagues and bring these problems to the attention of the appropriate person if you are not directly responsible for collection development. Remember to include resources for homework assignments in your library's collection development plan. Making use of the Internet and other online resources can help satisfy numerous student demands for succinct and timely materials. The acquisition of a particular reference book might be justified by the help it will give in providing homework support.

The Reference Interview

> "I need to find out exactly how many teenage girls who run away get abortions and how many use drugs."
>
> "I have to read a bibliography of Cleopatra for school."
>
> "I need a book that compares revenge in *Hamlet* with revenge in Stephen King's books."
>
> "Where are the books on history?"

Most homework support you provide to young adults will be in the context of reference work. And much of this work will involve the process known as the reference interview.

The primary goals of any reference interview are to determine what it is the patron really needs, how much information will meet that need, and what level of sophistication is appropriate for the patron. Once these determinations have been made, the librarian can help the patron access needed material intellectually and physically, as well as confirm that the patron has what is required.

Reference work in general has been called a "creative art," and the reference interview in particular a "performing art." To be sure, it is certainly more an art than a science. There are no exact formulas for a successful interview. Communication skills can be learned that are essential for effective interviewing. These include both verbal and nonverbal skills, such as

- making eye contact
- maintaining a relaxed posture
- using a concerned tone of voice
- remembering and sorting information
- avoiding premature assumptions about the patron or the question

- restating or paraphrasing
- using "encouragers"
- asking open-ended questions

Unless your advance preparations for providing homework support have enabled you to determine quickly in the reference interview what the young adult patron really wants, avoid jumping to conclusions. Experience suggests that few patrons ask for exactly what they need with the first question. The student searching for "books about Illinois" may really want a map of Chicago. You need to restate and paraphrase what is said during the interview and ask open-ended questions to help you determine the exact nature of the request.

Once you have defined the topic, it is very important for you to determine how much information is being requested. Perhaps the student who asks for "a book about the life of Martin Luther King" simply needs to answer a question about his dates of birth and death. A student working on a ten-page term paper will need more in-depth material than the one who is writing a one-page report. Here again, restating, paraphrasing, and asking open-ended questions will help define the request. Conduct a careful reference interview to determine the young adult's level of sophistication and match the student with materials appropriate to his or her level.

Many young adults are very literal, linear thinkers. You may need to help them consider alternative search strategies and sources. They may think that an assignment on X means that they have to find an entire book on X, and they don't think to check in more general sources for information that includes X. For example, a student approaches the reference desk and says, "I need to write a two-page report on Billy the Kid. I can't use encyclopedias, and everything you have about him is checked out!" You may need to suggest to the student that checking in more general sources on the Wild West or in histories of American crime might be productive. You may also discover during the reference interview that your patron has been trying to find information that simply cannot be found in your library—for example, data that either have not been collected or are unavailable, such as those needed for comparing the writing of two authors. You need to address this problem and help the student find what is available.

Occasionally, a student looking for a specific topic will know more about the general subject area than you do, such as a student who asks for information on covalent bonding. If you don't have adequate knowledge of the subject, admit your ignorance and ask the student to tell you more about it. This will help boost the student's self-confidence. It will also establish a participatory tone for the reference interview, and it may help you define a search strategy.

Always follow up the reference interview with a question such as "Is that what you were looking for?" to make sure that you've understood and adequately addressed the specific information need. Encouraging students to let you know if they need more help also lets them know that you're available if they run into problems in the research process.

Many people feel a certain degree of anxiety about using the library. Unlike most adult patrons, many young adults working on homework assignments are unenthusiastic about their research. The work has been assigned to them, and they may lack any motivation stronger than the fear of a failing grade. Sometimes they need you to take the first step and offer them assistance. They need you to be available, pleasant, helpful, interested, and to treat them and their questions with respect. By approaching the reference interview in this way, and by carefully conducting the interview, you can be of invaluable assistance.

Teaching Information Literacy

To what extent should the public librarian be concerned with instruction in information literacy skills? You may decide to work with local school library media specialists and offer group programs specifically to accomplish this purpose. However, it is widely believed that such skills are best learned when integrated into subjects being taught and when there is an immediate reason for learning them (that is, when there is a task that must be completed and the skills will help in the completion of that task). You may find that providing informal instruction while helping an individual student or small group of students is not only sufficient but more effective than providing bibliographic instruction to a group.

The American Association of School Librarians and the Association for Educational Communications and Technology have published *Information Literacy Standards for Student Learning*, which school and public librarians may use to measure students' success in accessing information.[11] A list of the basic standards is also published by AASL in handout form for distribution among educators, parents, and other interested community members. See "Information Literacy Standards for Student Learning" on page 124.

When working with a young adult or adult patron, talk about what you are doing and why. While you are using a catalog, bibliography, or electronic index, explain how it works—access points, cross-references, call numbers, citations, and so on. If you can take the time to escort the patron to the stacks to locate an item, do so and explain the physical layout of the stacks and shelf order. Even if the patron is not really interested in learning what you are explaining, some knowledge picked up will help the patron the next time there is a need to use the library.

There is a tendency for people to assume that because information is quick and easy to get via the Internet, that is generally the best source for obtaining information on all topics. It is the responsibility of librarians and teachers to educate students about the most appropriate search methods for different types of information. It is also important that students learn to critically evaluate the information they receive on the Web (and in print sources) in order to determine its credibility.

This type of instruction can be done unobtrusively by discussing issues of source and authority when assisting a patron in accessing information. Often, simply verbalizing the steps in a reference search helps teach patrons how they might conduct a search on their own. Find out what formal instruction the schools are providing in information literacy and make sure that public library instruction (whether formal or informal) complements the curriculum.

Above all, remember to follow up and verify. After your patrons have had time to select and examine some materials, ask if they have found something that completely answers their question. If they have not, offer additional assistance.

There are other matters you may need to address concerning how much work you are willing and able to do as you provide homework support—namely, the extent to which you will facilitate students' access to materials through interlibrary loan, the availability of telephone reference, and your ability and willingness to search online databases or to allow students to search for themselves. Any library policies regarding such matters should ensure equal access to resources for young adults.

One of the accepted goals of library service is "to save the time of the reader." To accomplish this in terms of providing homework support systems for your young adult patrons and to save your own scarce time, there are two things to keep in mind: preparation and communication. By preparing carefully and communicating clearly, you can make the experience of doing homework at the public library less frustrating for young adults and less taxing for yourself.

Programming

Popular Program Ideas

Author visits

Finals study break programs (music, munchies, and a place to study)

Game contests (traditional board games and role-playing games)

High school preparation programs (for junior high students and their parents)

Book and movie discussion programs (show the movie, talk about how it differs from the book it is based on)

Murder mysteries (written, directed, and performed by teens)

Library sleepovers (lock-ins)

College admissions and financial aid workshop (for high school students)

Trivia contests or "Battle of the Books"

Talent shows ("Battle of the Bands," etc.)

Summer reading

Babysitting workshops

Crafts (pottery, tie-dyes, jewelry making)

Cartooning workshops

Creative writing and poetry workshops

Coffeehouse and poetry slam

Summer job workshops

As of 1995, about half of all public libraries offered summer reading programs for young adults (57 percent) and 33 percent offered presentations and workshops on topics of interest to teenagers.[12] In addition to encouraging young adults to read, summer reading and listening programs promote use of the library's print and audiovisual resources. Presentations and workshops also meet young adult educational and recreational needs and promote a perception of the library as a cultural center of the community (see figure 6.4).

The key word in planning a young adult library program is preparation. Give yourself plenty of time before the date of the program to get all of the details in order. Some of the most successful program ideas are generated by teens themselves. Ask your Teen Advisory Board for ideas for program topics. They may even be able to suggest authors or workshop leaders who have great YA appeal. Continue to involve teens in all stages of planning by having them determine the structure and select the prizes for a YA summer reading program or plan the activities for a YA sleepover. If an outside speaker or presenter is involved, allow plenty of time to negotiate travel, lodging, honorarium, and scheduling. Get a commitment in writing specifying your expectations and the agreed-upon compensation. Don't forget to promote your event (with the assistance of YAs themselves) by placing ads in the local (and school) newspaper and on local TV and radio stations. Hang posters and flyers in the schools,

FIGURE 6.4   ▌ **The Why of YA Programming**

To attract young adults to the library

To introduce library services to the nonuser

To stimulate the use of library materials

To dramatize the services we offer and make the library a more inviting, interesting place for young adults

To encourage input and feedback about the library from teenagers

To establish the library and its staff as a dynamic and integral part of the community

To break down the barriers that keep some young people from using the library

To help YAs get through the process of being a YA

To support YAs in their quest for identity and to help them feel they belong

To provide a structure in which YAs can socialize and work together

To fill a void in the community

To provide an opportunity for YAs to assume responsibility

To introduce new ideas and broaden existing ones

To help YAs make the connection between their world and the library

Programs are alternative ways of providing information, education, and recreation.

Programs can be enriching and fun both for the librarian and the teenager.

Programs are important elements of total library service.

SOURCE: From "The Why of YA Programming" (A handout from Serving the Underserved, a seminar conducted by the Young Adult Library Services Association of the American Library Association, June 1994, in Miami, Florida), compiled by Judy Druse with input from numerous Serving the Underserved trainers.

library, and other venues in your community where teens hang out. Have teen volunteers on hand the night of the event to assist with preparation and cleanup. For some other ideas, see "Programming Tips" on page 126.

At the end of every YA program, allow time for students to complete a brief evaluation so that you will know what you did right and what you need to improve next time. Tailor the questions on your evaluation form to those aspects of the program for which you are most interested in feedback. Be sure to act on the suggestions you receive to improve future programs. For one example, see "Sample Young Adult Program Evaluation" on page 128.

Programming is often touted as an excellent way to get young adults into the library. Always promoting topical library materials at YA programs is also an excellent way to encourage use of the library's collections. Perhaps most importantly, enjoyable events promote a perception among teens that the library is an interesting and exciting place. They also give the young adult librarian an excellent opportunity to meet and interact with teens who might not ordinarily use the library's resources, which may lead to discoveries about how to better serve this segment of the population.

Outreach

Public libraries have much to contribute and gain by cooperation with other agencies serving youth. Although most libraries cooperate with schools to some extent, "Libraries with medium to large numbers of patrons and those with a young adult or youth specialist were more likely to work with [other] organizations than libraries serving fewer than two hundred patrons per week and those without a youth specialist."[13] Yet smaller libraries and those without a young adult specialist might have more to gain by reaching out to other agencies that serve teens in their community.

Attending association board meetings or community events is a good way to begin networking with other organizations in your area. Representatives from many agencies would also be happy to meet with you individually to discuss their activities and provide a tour of their facilities, and you could offer to do the same at the library. Dana Burton of the Monroe County (Ind.) Public Library had an innovative approach to networking with other youth services workers in her community—she invited them all to a sleepover at the library to discuss ideas and strategies for working with youth!

Librarians have long provided class visits to the library to teach students about their resources in particular areas. The same principle can be extended to other agencies that serve youth. Public librarians could also offer to visit the schools

Percentage of Public Libraries That Cooperate with Other Organizations Serving Young Adults

schools (76%)

youth organizations (54%)

at-risk programs (27%)

health or mental health agencies (23%)

cultural institutions (19%)

recreational institutions (17%)

correctional facilities (9%)[14]

and other organizations to conduct booktalks, tell stories, or promote library use. Many middle school, junior high, and high school teachers have misconceptions about young adult literature, based in part on their opinions of the paperback series displays in the young adult sections of bookstores. Public librarians can team up with school library media specialists to introduce teachers to the variety of high-quality young adult literature that is available and appropriate for use in the classroom. For "How to Write Your Own Booktalk" and for "Tips on Booktalking to a Group," see pages 117 and 118.

Other agencies have expertise in areas of youth services that libraries may not be as knowledgeable about. For example, the parks and recreation department can alert you to recreational events open to teens within the community, local hospitals may be able to provide information about teen health issues, and arts and cultural organizations may sponsor contests or scholarships for young adults.

It is essential that in contacts with outside agencies we emphasize not only what they can do for us, but also what we can do for them. When cooperatively planning programs and activities or sharing resources, the emphasis should always be on collaboration and on the mutual benefits of working together.

Some libraries set up deposit collections in school classrooms, community centers, juvenile detention centers, and even in commercial businesses such as cafes, bagel shops, and arcades that serve teens. Sharing resources may also take the form of interlibrary loan, automation projects, or shared online resources.

Some of the most successful examples of interagency cooperation involve programming. Commercial businesses often team up with public libraries to promote summer reading. Libraries and other agencies that serve youth can cosponsor programs and activities that are likely to increase the use of both organizations. Many grants require cooperation between community agencies and encourage the sharing of resources (see figure 6.5).

One of the greatest benefits of working closely with other community organizations is improving your awareness of the services available to young adults in your area. This will help

FIGURE 6.5 ▌ Libraries and Bookstores as a Power Alliance for Reading

Let's Collaborate!

Get Together, Plan a Regional Meeting

Contacts

> At public libraries: the librarian responsible for serving young adults
>
> At school libraries: the school library media specialist
>
> At bookstores: the children's manager and the community relations coordinator

Share Resources, Expertise

> Bookstores have a cool social space, a finger on the pulse of young adult book buying, freedom from censorship pressures, free speakers, and program resources from publishers.
>
> Libraries have resources and background knowledge, out-of-print and reference titles as well as current books, and expertise in working with kids
>
> School libraries have a captive audience.

Libraries and Bookstores Can—and Do—Collaborate!

> By displaying each other's events calendars.
>
> By sharing speakers, character costumes, and publishers' materials.
>
> By working together with teachers.
>
> By sharing teen peer book reviewing.
>
> By cosponsoring major events such as Banned Books Week programs.
>
> By working together on school book fairs.
>
> By joining together to publicize national book awards.
>
> By providing booktalking and lists of recommended titles and resources (libraries) and data on popular teen reading and multiple copies at a discount for reading groups (bookstores).
>
> By respecting each other's abilities and commitment to quality teen reading.

SOURCE: http://www.ala.org/yalsa/professional/bookstores.html

you in referring young adult patrons to the agencies best designed to meet their needs. It will also provide the library with useful information created and distributed by these organizations. Additionally, it will increase the library's visibility within the community and encourage other organizations to refer their young adults to you.

NOTES

1. Ana Marie Cox, "Wasted on the Young," FEEDLINE (http://www.feedmag.com/html/home.html), July 10, 1998.

2. U.S. Department of Education, Office of Educational Research and Improvement, National Center for Education Statistics, *Services and Resources for Children and Young Adults in Public Libraries* (Washington, D.C.: U.S. Government Printing Office, 1995), 56.

3. Laura Zinn with Jonathan Berry et al., "Teens: Here Comes the Biggest Wave Yet," *Business Week*, April 14, 1994, p. 79.

4. Ibid., 82.

5. Ibid., 84.

6. C. Allen Nichols, "Merchandising YA Collections" (A handout from Serving the Underserved II, a seminar conducted by the Young Adult Library Services Association of the American Library Association, January 1996, in San Antonio, Texas).

7. American Association of School Librarians and Association for Educational Communications and Technology, *Information Power: Building Partnerships for Learning* (Chicago: American Library Assn., 1998).

8. American Association of School Librarians and Association for Educational Communications and Technology, *Information Literacy Standards for Student Learning* (Chicago: American Library Assn., 1998).

9. Ibid.

10. U.S. Department of Education, Office of Educational Research and Improvement, National Center for Education Statistics, *Services and Resources for Children and Young Adults in Public Libraries* (Washington, D.C.: U.S. Government Printing Office, 1995), 43.

11. *Information Literacy Standards.*

12. U.S. Department of Education, Office of Educational Research and Improvement, National Center for Education Statistics, *Services and Resources for Children and Young Adults in Public Libraries* (Washington, D.C.: U.S. Government Printing Office, 1995), 43.

13. Ibid., 49.

14. Ibid.

7

Rights and Responsibilities

Intellectual Freedom

"Libraries, acting within their mission and objectives, must support access to information on all subjects that serve the needs or interests of each user, regardless of the user's age or the content of the material."[1]

ALA policies are very clear about the fact that young adults deserve the same service and the same access to service as any other group using the library. Basically, there are three things to keep in mind:

1. It is up to the child and his or her parent to determine what material is appropriate for him or her.

2. The librarian may not impose his or her own personal or moral views on people seeking information.

3. Individual parents cannot speak for any children but their own.

Nearly all intellectual freedom problems in public libraries concerning young adults originate from misunderstandings over these three issues. It is important to be able to speak with people intelligently about them. Remember that the young adult is your primary client, even when requesting information that is upsetting to you or someone else. As long as what young adults want is within the scope of the public library to provide, they have a right to it, free from the interference of others including the librarian.

The best way to cope with intellectual freedom challenges is to be familiar enough with both the ALA's and your own library's policies regarding the role of the public library in society and youth access to information in order to be able to explain them to your adult and young adult patrons.

It is important to remain courteously attentive to anyone who complains to you about young adult resources or services. Demonstrating through your body language your respect for that person's right to a viewpoint different from that of library policy is a great way to model tolerance for diverse viewpoints. This is important under all circumstances, but especially when the person is discussing his or her own children or when the complaint involves an issue of perceived insensitivity. Under no circumstances do you want to inadvertently convey the impression that you do not believe the person is raising his or her adolescent child(ren) properly. Nor do you want to imply that you agree with something the person feels demeans his or her race, sex, ethnicity, or disability—all of which are life circumstances over which the person has no control. This can be particularly difficult if you happen to agree with the person complaining to you or if the person is aggravating in some way.

Regardless of your personal opinion, the librarian's role is primarily to explain library policy. You may say something like, "It's great that you take an interest in what your child is reading. Reading is often a very good way not only to promote discussion with your teenager but also to convince him or her that reading is important to you." Having established a communal basis for discussion, you may continue, "The library is a public forum that provides many different viewpoints on human activity. We recognize that not everyone will agree with everything here, but our role is to assure that a broad variety of materials is available from which you can choose. What you and your child choose is exactly that—*your* choice. It is not the role of a government agency such as the library to come between you and your child."

After explaining the library's policy, you might want to offer to help the person find something more in line with their sensibilities. Ask if there are titles more representative of that person's viewpoint that she or he might want to recommend for library purchase and be sure to follow through on any suggestions you get. Be prepared to show the person written policies that support what you have explained verbally. If your library has a "Request for Reconsideration" form or policy, you might want to make that available to the patron as well. If the patron would like to speak to a supervisor, facilitate that contact. Often having someone in authority repeat what you have said is a good way to convey the message.

If the person becomes verbally or physically abusive, walk away and call a supervisor immediately. While library policies may vary, no public service staff member should be expected to endure abuse. Try, however, to remain calm. It is never clear with these encounters whether you are dealing with a single upset person or with the first foray of an attack by an organized censorship group. One thing that is clear, though, is that the public service desk is almost inevitably the first point of contact for a complaint. If it is only an individual whose personal value system is affronted, your behavior when the person approaches you may make the difference between whether that person goes away feeling that she or he has been heard or organizes with others to launch an attack on an organization that they feel treated them badly.

Many librarians grapple with whether to include popular adult materials in the young adult collection. In determining the scope of your YA collection, consider your library's mission and service responses. A library that adopts the service response of Current Topics and Titles would want to include adult materials that are in high demand by teens. If your library has adopted the Library Bill of Rights as part of its policy, keep these principles in mind when selecting materials for your young adult collection. Restricted collections and labeling possibly offensive material are not considered in keeping with the principles of the Library Bill of Rights. See page 129 for the "Library Bill of Rights."

Young adults should also have unrestricted access to materials in other collections and in all formats. The same intellectual freedom principles that apply to books should also apply to audiovisual and electronic media. For the text of the ALA's statement on "The Freedom to Read," see page 130.

The American Library Association has affirmed that "the use of filtering software by libraries to block access to constitutionally protected speech violates the Library Bill of Rights."[4] Teens are particularly vulnerable to

The use in libraries of software filters which block constitutionally protected speech is inconsistent with the United States Constitution and federal law and may lead to legal exposure for the library and its governing authorities.[2]

Libraries and librarians should not deny or limit access to information available via electronic resources because of its allegedly controversial content or because of the librarian's personal beliefs or fear of confrontation.[3]

efforts to impose restrictions on Internet access, since they often need information about topics considered to be controversial in order to complete school assignments or simply to weigh both sides of an issue before developing a personal opinion about it. Efforts to "protect" younger children from information that requires more maturity to understand are often inappropriately applied to teens as well.

Confidentiality guidelines that apply to a patron's borrowing records should apply to their use of electronic and other library resources as well. All efforts should be made to eliminate any record of what information is being accessed by a particular patron on the library's computer resources.

Your library's policy should clearly state its stance on sharing information about a minor's borrowing history with a parent or allowing a parent to cancel the minor's card if the parent is financially responsible for fines and lost book fees. Both parent and child should be aware of this policy at the time they apply for a library card. This policy should be consistent with state and federal laws about confidentiality of library records and in keeping with the spirit of your library's stance on intellectual freedom.

> Library use of blocking/filtering software creates an implied contract with parents that their children *will not* be able to access material on the Internet that they do not wish their children to read or view. Libraries will be unable to fulfill this implied contract, due to the technological limitations of the software, thus exposing themselves to possible legal liability and litigation.[5]

> Users have both the right of confidentiality and the right of privacy. The library should uphold these rights by policy, procedure, and practice.[6]

If you involve young adults in the creation of newsletters, host writing contests, or provide other forums for youth publication, it is important to apply the principles of intellectual freedom to these publications as well as those you select for your collection. Although the library certainly has the right (perhaps even an obligation) to determine the scope or purpose of a library-sponsored publication and to establish guidelines for submission, entries should not be censored based solely on their content. It is the responsibility of teachers and librarians to instruct students in the most appropriate means of communicating their opinions for publication. It is not the role of teachers and librarians to influence or censor those opinions.

> The script to "Don't Read This," a play written by members of the Boulder Public Library's Young Adult Advisory Board to raise awareness of censorship issues, appears as an appendix in *Youth Participation in School and Public Libraries: It Works* (YALSA, 1995).

Banned Books Week is an excellent event to celebrate with young adults. Many teens are fascinated to learn that some of their favorite books have been challenged or removed from school or public library collections due to partisan or doctrinal disapproval. Consider involving teens in the creation of displays or events to celebrate Banned Books Week. They are the best advocates for explaining why access to a wide variety of materials is so important to them during this crucial stage of their lives.

Troubleshooting

Adolescents behave like the adult society that raises them. They did not land on a meteorite. We raised them. They share our values. They act like us. When we criticize their behaviors, we are really engaging in devastating self-criticism without a mirror.[7]

Since few libraries are set up with young adults primarily in mind, normal adolescent behavior can often lead frustrated or frightened librarians to consider YAs to be troublemakers. A disruptive teenager can be unnerving, but most perceptions of young adults as troublemakers in libraries stem from unrealistic library regulations, frightened staff, or prejudicial attitudes toward youth. A few rules of thumb for coping with young adult behavior include

1. Understand what constitutes normal adolescent behavior.
2. Make sure your library has a written behavior policy that is equitably enforced.
3. Explain the reasons behind the rules.
4. Explain the consequences of continuing inappropriate behavior and enforce those consequences.
5. Involve young adults themselves in finding solutions to problems.
6. Call law enforcement to intervene if the behavior is illegal or becomes dangerous.

Although adolescents are no more likely to engage in inappropriate behavior than are adults or children, there are certain types of problem behavior that adolescents (due to developmental stages or peer pressure) may engage in more frequently. Following are examples of young adult behaviors that may cause problems within the library. Many of these behaviors may be engaged in by adults or children as well, and it is important to enforce rules and the consequences of breaking those rules equitably regardless of the age of the patron.

Loud or Rowdy Behavior

Normal healthy teenagers travel in groups. Any large group of people talking can be disruptive in a library. Young adults are often so involved with each other that they do not realize that they are disturbing other people. Also, adolescent culture is much more tolerant of noise than are people over thirty, which include many librarians. Most of the time, if teenagers are asked to quiet down, they will cooperate. The noise level will go down for a while but it may rise again because the teens are still talking and still oblivious to those around them. As long as they are not destructive or disruptive to others, another reminder to quiet down will usually be sufficient. It is important for you to realize that this behavior is normal; the kids are not doing it deliberately to annoy you.

"Hogging" the Internet

Whether teens are using the Internet for e-mail, chat, or research, they may lose track of time when engrossed in what they are doing on the computer. If your library sets time limits on computer use, those limits should be enforced equitably regardless of the age of the patron or the sites that she or he chooses to access.

Vandalism and Theft

Although vandalism and theft are not committed solely by teens, graffiti, theft, and mutilation of library materials are often blamed on young adults. Providing teens with appropriate outlets for expression such as newsletters and bulletin boards may cut down on graffiti in the library. I have found that making teens aware of the consequences of theft or mutilation of library materials often deters incidents from occurring. For example, a note on the magazine shelf explaining that the current issue of *Seventeen* magazine is not available because it was stolen may make teens think twice about the effects of their actions.

Smoking

Many libraries don't allow smoking on their grounds. Teens who are at risk of suspension or expulsion for smoking on school grounds may find it tempting to light up on library property after school. Rules about smoking should be enforced equitably with teenage patrons and adults.

Skateboarding

In many towns and cities, skateboarders have very few places where they can safely practice their sport. Often, library sidewalks and parking lots are used as skate parks. If skateboarding on your library's grounds poses a risk to the skateboarders or to other patrons using the building, your library may choose to set restrictions on skateboarding on library grounds. Such guidelines should not be more restrictive than necessary. If it is safe for students to skate in a particular area on the library grounds, the library may not need to ban skateboarding altogether.

Violence and Drug Use

Incidents of violence, drug use, or other illegal activity on library grounds should be reported to law enforcement immediately. At no time should librarians put themselves at risk in order to attempt to control the actions of a threatening or dangerous patron, regardless of his or her age.

Make sure that adolescents understand the reasons for the rules you have established in your library. Explaining to them that their behavior is disruptive to others helps them understand that your motivation is not primarily to persecute them. Also, make sure that young adults understand what the consequences will be if they continue their inappropriate behavior, and remember to enforce those consequences.

"American teenagers," reports Public Agenda's executive director Deborah Wadsworth, "hunger for structure, discipline, and more rigorous standards. They complain bitterly about lax instructors and unenforced rules. Many feel insulted at the minimal demands placed upon them. They state unequivocally that they would work harder if more were expected of them."[8]

I like to use a "three strikes" rule. The first time I approach disruptive patrons I explain how their behavior is being disruptive and ask them to change it. If I have to intervene again, I explain that if the behavior doesn't stop, I will have to take more drastic action. Depending on your library policies, this could mean asking YAs to separate or to leave the library. The third step of the "three strikes" rule is the most important, and that is to enforce the consequences that you identified in the second reminder. Failure to do so will result in a loss of respect for your authority on the part of the teens, and they will continue to behave inappropriately regardless of what you say or do to make them stop.

Any behavior policy that your library creates should be equitably enforced with patrons of all ages. The "three strikes" rule works just as well with adults as young adults. It is important to avoid stereotyping YAs and expecting them to misbehave in the library. As numerous scientific studies have shown, people generally live up to the expectations that others set for them. See page 135 for "Strategies for Dealing with Troublesome Behavior."

NOTES

1. American Library Association, Intellectual Freedom Committee, "Access to Electronic Information, Services and Networks: An Interpretation of the Library Bill of Rights," adopted by the ALA Council, January 24, 1996.

2. Ibid.

3. Ibid.

4. American Library Association, Intellectual Freedom Committee, "Statement on Library Use of Filtering Software," July 1, 1997.

5. Ibid.

6. American Library Association, Intellectual Freedom Committee, "Access to Electronic Information."

7. Mike A. Males, "Debunking 10 Myths about Teens," *Education Digest*, December 1997, p. 48.

8. Diane Ravitch, "What Do Teenagers Want?" *Forbes*, October 20, 1997, p. 224.

Continuing Education for Improved Service

Staff Training

It is not enough for you to know all that you need to know about working with adolescents. It is important that everyone on the library staff has an awareness of young adult developmental needs and behaviors. You can encourage staff YA awareness through posting articles of interest on the staff bulletin board, doing presentations about young adult services at staff meetings, and highlighting YA events and activities in the staff and library newsletter. At least once a year you should plan a staff in-service training on some aspect of young adult services. If you do not feel qualified to conduct such training seek local experts through your network of community contacts or through your state or regional library association. YALSA has developed a database of presenters who have training in conducting workshops and presentations on young adult services. A database of contact information for these trainers is included on the YALSA Web site at www.ala.org/yalsa/professional/trainersmain.html

Local Involvement

Even if you are the only library serving your community, there are probably numerous continuing education opportunities available in your area that are sponsored by other organizations.

Be on the lookout for classes and lectures on adolescent development and behavior. These are often sponsored by hospitals or mental health agencies and frequently target an audience of parents of teenagers. The local YMCA or YWCA and the schools may offer similar programs. If there don't seem to be many relevant events in your community, consider offering one of your own. Parents, teachers, and other youth leaders may have a lot to learn about young adult reading interests and informational needs that you are in an excellent position to discuss. Some libraries have used parent-child book discussion groups as a forum to encourage honest communication between generations in families about the issues affecting their lives.

State and Regional Involvement

Most state and regional library associations have a division that deals with children's and young adult services. These associations usually host conferences at which workshops and presentations are held on a wide variety of issues related to young adult services. These organizations are often able to entice national or regional experts in the field or young adult authors to speak about their work. State and regional conferences also provide an excellent opportunity to meet other young adult librarians in your area. Once these connections have been established, you may want to set up visits to some other libraries in your area that serve young adults to see what kinds of services they offer that are successful and to share some of your own ideas and experiences.

Some state library agencies, such as the Office of Library and Information Services in Rhode Island, sponsor monthly meetings at which young adult librarians, consultants, and library school students gather to exchange ideas and information relating to YA materials, programs, and services. If such a gathering is impractical in your area, you might consider starting a newsletter or electronic discussion list, or instituting roundtable discussions at your annual state or regional library conferences through which to exchange information. Library schools and local colleges also may offer continuing education and workshops in young adult literature or services.

National Involvement

YALSA Vision Statement

In every library in the nation, quality library service to young adults is provided by a staff that understands and respects the unique informational, educational, and recreational needs of teenagers. Equal access to information, services, and materials is recognized as a right, not a privilege. Young adults are actively involved in the library decision-making process. The library staff collaborates and cooperates with other youth-serving agencies to provide a holistic, community-wide network of activities and services that support healthy youth development.

The Young Adult Library Services Association (YALSA) within ALA is the most relevant unit for information about young adult resources, services, and programs. Its goal is to advocate, promote, and strengthen service to young adults, ages twelve through eighteen, as part of the continuum of total library services.

The Public Library Association (PLA) within ALA enhances the development and effectiveness of public librarians and public library services. This mission positions PLA to focus its efforts on serving the needs of its members, address issues that affect public libraries, promote and protect the profession, and commit to quality public library services that benefit the general public.

Getting involved on the national level is an excellent way to make contact with people who are doing some of the most exciting library work in the country. Aside from observation and interaction with teens themselves, professional colleagues are the best source of information about the field. Attending a national conference can give you a fresh perspective and provide you with inspiration when you lack enthusiasm or new ideas. You may also have the opportunity to meet some of your favorite YA authors and to get a sneak preview of the next releases from your favorite publishing houses.

Advocacy

Youth advocacy in libraries is the support or defense of the rights of youth to equal access of information, resources, and services in all libraries.[1]

Since most teens do not contribute to the economy by working full time (although many have part-time jobs) and are not yet old enough to vote, their rights, interests, and needs are often overlooked or disregarded in the library and

Teen Library Council Testimony

For me the library was always a symbol of refuge and peace. I grew up going to [libraries] constantly (my mother was a former librarian). In high school, I often went to the back corner by the window just to get away from everything and immerse myself in another world. And in college, it is the only place of quiet. The [Teen Library] Council and volunteering helped me take a more active role in actually helping the library. Books *are* a mirror for the soul; the good ones expose every detail of humanity to you. It is even grotesque sometimes at how closely we are shown. Yet they also reflect our emotions of joy and amazingly can even cause it; in fact the good ones take you through a journey of exposing grotesque detail that results in exuberant, cathartic joy. While all art reveals this journey, books are unique because you invest time, a fraction of your life, to someone else's world. It is so intense because it is so involved.[4]

in society. The stereotypes about teens based on their appearance or a misunderstanding of teen culture often puts young adults in a disadvantaged position. It is the responsibility of adults working with teens to advocate on their behalf. This may mean providing teens their right to free speech in the library newsletter or defending their right to access a wide variety of materials in the library. Since teens are not in a position of power in most organizations, they depend on adults to argue and defend their causes or to pave the way for their voices to be heard. Sometimes it can take a great deal of courage to stand up against adults who believe that they have the best interest of "children" in mind. But ultimately every teen, with guidance from his or her parents, will have to decide what is appropriate for himself or herself, and the freedom to make this choice will provide teens with the skills they need to function effectively in an adult world.

Mary K. Chelton and Dorothy Broderick propagated the concept of youth advocacy in young adult librarianship by naming their review journal *Voice of Youth Advocates* (VOYA) in 1978. Broderick stated that "a youth advocate is a person who believes in creating the conditions under which young people can make decisions about their own lives."[2] In this context, youth advocacy goes hand in hand with youth participation to drive young adult library services. In the words of current VOYA editor Cathi Dunn MacRae, "It takes a youth advocate to practice youth participation."[3] Youth advocacy, in its truest sense, is not about adults speaking for minors, but about adults paving the way for teens to speak for themselves and to be heard (see figure 8.1).

FIGURE 8.1
  Definition of Youth Advocacy

What intellectual rights do young people have? Adults answering this question approach the issue from one of two positions: as protectors of youth or as advocates of youth.

In the role of protector, the assumption is that the adult knows what is best for youth, what will harm them, what information needs they have, and how those needs can be met. These adults protect youth from themselves, others, and ideas. The stance is limiting, restricting access to what is perceived as best or appropriate for young library users. The result is that librarians develop collections based on what is expected to elicit the least amount of parental and societal displeasure. The protector seeks to limit the resources made available to youth and erects barriers between youth and information, thereby retaining power over them.

The role of advocate assumes an open stance. From this perspective adults view youth as capable of defining their information needs and capable of making judgments about what is best for them. Adults assume a responsibility to empower youth to identify, retrieve, and use information, and they seek to expand the resources made available to youth, promote access, and encourage exploration of ideas. These advocates remove barriers between youth and information.

SOURCE: Frances McDonald, "Information Access for Youth: Issues and Concerns," *Library Trends* (summer 1988): 50.

NOTES

1. YALSA, "Definitions of Youth Advocacy" (from Serving the Underserved II, a seminar conducted by the Young Adult Library Services Association of the American Library Association, January 1996, in San Antonio, Texas), 2-6.

2. Dorothy Broderick, *Top of the News* 35 (spring 1979): 223.

3. Cathi Dunn MacRae, e-mail correspondence, October 26, 1998.

4. Cristi Booth, Teen Library Council Member (vice president 1996–97), Carmel Clay (Ind.) Public Library.

Conclusion

Kids, because of demographics, have far less access to time with adults than in previous eras, and . . . time invested in them in the few moments we interact with them in libraries is precious and shouldn't be wasted. Given the social indicators for the age group, we should be part of the solution, not part of the problem.[1]

When Scott Adams, the cartoonist who creates the Dilbert comic strip, was just starting out, he saw the closing credits for a PBS television show about cartooning and contacted the host, Jack Cassady, about how he might get started in the cartooning field. Cassady sent him a letter encouraging him to submit his work to some of the magazines listed in *Artist's Market* and reminding him not to give up in the face of rejection. Adams chose the two magazines that paid the most (*Playboy* and *New Yorker*) and sent them samples of his work. Both of his submissions were rejected. He ignored Cassady's advice and decided that he wasn't meant to be a cartoonist.

Over a year later, he received another letter from Cassady, completely unbidden, asking if Adams had submitted his work to any magazines and reminding him again not to give up. It was that second letter that encouraged Adams to submit his comic strips to the major cartoon syndicates, which launched the birth of Dilbert. If that one person hadn't gone the extra mile, the working world would be a little bit less funny today.

The truth of the matter is that we never know how our actions will affect people. Young adults who come into the public library are often experiencing a difficult transition in their lives. They are accustomed to being treated with suspicion and distrust. Effective young adult services are in everyone's best interest, from the Board of Trustees and the Director down to the library staff and the kids themselves. A little bit of kindness on the part of librarians and other adults can go a long way toward helping teens find their way in the world. And you never know what might happen if you decide to go that extra mile.

NOTE

1. Mary K. Chelton, associate professor, Graduate School of Library and Information Studies, Queens College, Flushing, New York.

By-Laws for the Louisville Public Library Teen Advisory Board

ARTICLE I: Name

This organization shall be called "The Teen Advisory Board of the Louisville Public Library" and abbreviated as "TAB."

ARTICLE II: Mission

The mission of the TAB is to promote Louisville Public Library's services to young adults by

Planning and implementing young adult programs

Creating an inviting atmosphere at the library by maintaining a safe, attractive young adult area

Promoting ideas in the young adult collection

Promoting and encouraging reading by young adults

Advocating the rights of young adults

ARTICLE III: Membership

Section 1

TAB shall be coordinated by an adult volunteer or library staff member who will supervise all **TAB** meetings, activities, and special projects.

Section 2

TAB shall consist of no more than twenty-five members. Members will be accepted to the board based on the following criteria:

Availability of a seat on **TAB**

Quotas from area schools

Quality of responses on TAB application

Section 3

TAB membership is open to young adults in grades 6 through 12. Members must have a valid Louisville Public Library card (or a card issued from another eligible library) that is in good standing (no excessive fines as described by the Library's policy). TAB members with fines must make an effort to rectify the matter.

Section 4

TAB members must have parental permission to join the board. Members will be given specific permission slips for specific TAB activities (field trips, special projects) that will need to be turned in before a member can participate.

Section 5

Membership shall commence at the next TAB meeting after being accepted on the board and will continue until member graduates from high school or reaches nineteen years of age, whichever is last.

Section 6

A member shall become "inactive" after two unexcused absences. Active members will have unexcused absences pardoned after six months. Inactive members will not be informed of meetings or provided minutes from meetings. Inactive members will no longer be eligible to vote or participate in TAB activities. An absence shall be considered unexcused when a member is absent from an official TAB meeting and makes no effort to inform the TAB Coordinator. It is solely up to the TAB Coordinator to decide if an absence is excused or unexcused.

Section 7

When membership is available, the TAB Coordinator and current members will actively recruit new members.

ARTICLE IV: Officers
Section 1

The officers shall be a president, a vice-president, a secretary, and a treasurer, elected from the members of TAB. All officers should make a special effort to attend all meetings, programs, and special events sponsored by TAB.

Section 2

The president of TAB will work closely with the TAB Coordinator to organize TAB meetings. The president will assist the TAB Coordinator in creating the meeting agenda and will preside over TAB meetings. The president will act as a contact person for other TAB members who want items added to the meeting agenda.

Section 3

The vice-president will serve as the president in his or her absence. The vice-president will serve as membership coordinator, keeping track of active and inactive members and new applications. The vice-president will inform and remind all members of upcoming meetings, programs, and special events.

Section 4

The secretary will keep minutes of TAB meetings, providing copies to each member in a timely fashion. The secretary will inform the vice-president of members absent at meetings. The secretary will read the previous meeting's minutes at each regular meeting. The secretary will see to the upkeep of the master file of minutes to be kept in the TAB basket. The secretary will serve as the president in the absence of the presiding president and vice-president.

Section 5

The treasurer will keep track of any TAB income or expenditures. The treasurer will keep track of all TAB supplies in the TAB basket. The treasurer will track the cost of TAB meetings, young adult programs, and special events by keeping track of time spent on projects, supplies used, and other expenditures. The treasurer will act as the president in the absence of other officers, and will act as secretary in his or her absence.

Section 6

Officers will serve a term of one year, from September to the following August, based on the school calendar year.

Section 7

Each August, a new election will be held. Officers may not serve in the same office two years in a row, although they may run for and be elected to a different office. A member may run for and be elected to a previously held office after one year of not holding that office. The exception will be for the officers elected the first term (1998-1999), who will be allowed to run for re-election for the same office if they so choose, since the first term of office will be shorter than one year.

Section 8

In order for an election to be final, ballots must be turned in by at least two-thirds of members.

ARTICLE V: Meetings

Section 1

The regular meetings will be held once a month, the date and hour to be decided at the previous meeting.

Section 2

Special meetings may be called by the TAB coordinator to complete tasks as needed.

Section 3

Minutes of the previous meeting shall be mailed to all active members within a week of the meeting. Members will be provided with a folder to store their minutes and are required to bring copies of the minutes to each meeting. A master copy of all minutes will be kept in a folder in the TAB basket in case any member loses any copies of the minutes.

Section 4

Proceedings of meetings should be governed by *Robert's Rules of Order.*

ARTICLE VI: Committees

The following committees shall be coordinated by a TAB member appointed by the TAB Coordinator. Each committee will be made up of volunteer TAB members.

  a. Young Adult Area Upkeep and Filing Committee—which shall see to the organization and upkeep of the young adult stacks and new book display area, as well as specific tasks as assigned.

b. Newsletter Committee—which shall coordinate and contribute to a quarterly young adult newsletter to be distributed to the library and to area schools.

c. Louisville *Herald* Committee—which shall remain in contact with the local newspaper and provide regular articles and news releases to promote the young adult collection, TAB activities, and young adult programs.

ARTICLE VII: Code of Ethics

Section 1

TAB members will keep the TAB Mission at the forefront of all TAB activities.

Section 2

During all TAB meetings, activities, and library functions, TAB members will act in a way that reflects positively on the Louisville Public Library.

Section 3

TAB members will show respect for other TAB members, library staff and library patrons. Members will demonstrate respect for others by listening attentively when someone else is speaking, asking questions when clarification is needed, and by refraining from negative comments when responding to other people's ideas.

Section 4

TAB members will show respect for library materials and property by taking care to leave meeting spaces neat and orderly.

Section 5

TAB members will strive to make use of their time during meetings and while working on projects by staying on task.

Section 6

TAB members will respect the privacy of other TAB members.

ARTICLE VIII: Removal of Members from TAB

In the extremely rare case that a member of TAB is consistently disruptive to the mission of TAB, it is the responsibility of the TAB Coordinator to remove that person from membership. The TAB Coordinator will make every attempt to resolve the situation without removing a member from the Board.

SOURCE: Maureen T. Lerch, Young Adult Librarian, Orrville (Ohio) Public Library

Young Adults Deserve the Best: YALSA Competencies for Librarians Serving Youth

AREA I—Leadership and Professionalism

The librarian will be able to:

1. Develop and demonstrate leadership skills in articulating a program of excellence for young adults.

2. Exhibit planning and evaluating skills in the development of a comprehensive program for young adults.

3. Develop and demonstrate a commitment to professionalism.

   a. Adhere to the American Library Association Code of Ethics.

   b. Demonstrate a non-judgmental attitude toward young adults.

   c. Preserve confidentiality in interactions with young adults.

4. Plan for personal and professional growth and career development through active participation in professional associations and continuing education.

5. Develop and demonstrate a strong commitment to the right of young adults to have physical and intellectual access to information that is consistent with the American Library Association's Library Bill of Rights.

6. Demonstrate an understanding of and a respect for diversity in cultural and ethnic values.

7. Encourage young adults to become lifelong library users by helping them to discover what libraries have to offer and how to use libraries.

AREA II—Knowledge of Client Group

The librarian will be able to:

1. Apply factual and interpretative information on adolescent psychology, growth and development, sociology,

and popular culture in planning for materials, services and programs for young adults.

2. Apply knowledge of the reading process and of types of reading problems in the development of collections and programs for young adults.

3. Identify the special needs of discrete groups of young adults and design and implement programs and build collections appropriate to their needs.

AREA III—Communication

The librarian will be able to:

1. Demonstrate effective interpersonal relations with young adults, administrators, other professionals who work with young adults, and the community at large by:

   a. Using principles of group dynamics and group process.
   b. Establishing regular channels of communication, both written and oral, with each group.

2. Apply principles of effective communication which reinforce positive behaviors in young adults.

AREA IV—Administration

A. PLANNING

The librarian will be able to:

1. Develop a strategic plan for library service to young adults.

   a. Formulate goals, objectives, and methods of evaluation for a young adult program based on determined needs.
   b. Design and conduct a community analysis and needs assessment.
   c. Apply research findings for the development and improvement of the young adult program.
   d. Design, conduct, and evaluate local action research for program improvement.

2. Design, implement, and evaluate an ongoing public relations and report program directed toward young adults, administrators, boards, staff, other agencies serving young adults, and the community at large.

3. Identify and cooperate with other information agencies in networking arrangements to expand access to information for young adults.

4. Develop, justify, administer, and evaluate a budget for the young adult program.

5. Develop physical facilities which contribute to the achievement of young adult program goals.

B. MANAGING

The librarian will be able to:

1. Supervise and evaluate other staff members who work with young adults.

2. Design, implement and evaluate an ongoing program of professional development.

3. Develop policies and procedures for the efficient operation of all technical functions, including acquisition, processing, circulation, collection maintenance, equipment supervision, and scheduling of young adult programs.

4. Identify external sources of funding and other support and apply for those suitable for the young adult program.

5. Monitor legislation and judicial decisions pertinent to young adults, especially those that affect youth rights, and disseminate this information.

AREA V—Knowledge of Materials

The librarian will be able to:

1. Formulate collection development and selection policies for young adult materials, consistent with the parent institution's policies.

2. Using a broad range of selection sources, develop a collection of materials for young adults that includes all appropriate formats.

3. Demonstrate a knowledge and appreciation of literature for young adults.

4. Identify current reading, viewing, and listening interests of young adults and incorporate these findings into collection development and programs.

5. Design and locally produce materials in a variety of formats to expand the collections.

6. Incorporate new and improved technology (e.g., computers and software, digitized information, video, the Internet and the World Wide Web) into young adult collections and programs.

7. Maintain awareness of ongoing technological advances and a minimum level of expertise with electronic resources.

AREA VI—Access to Information

The librarian will be able to:

1. Organize collections to guarantee easy and equitable access to information for young adults.

2. Use current standard methods of cataloging and classification, as well as incorporate the newest means of electronic access to information.

3. Create an environment which attracts and invites young adults to use the collection.

4. Develop special tools which provide access to information not readily available, (e.g., community resources, special collections, and links to appropriate and useful websites).

5. Create and disseminate promotional materials that will ease access to collections and motivate their use.

AREA VII—Services

The librarian will be able to:

1. Utilize a variety of techniques (e.g., booktalking, discussion groups) to encourage use of materials.

2. Provide a variety of information services (e.g., career information, homework help, web sites) to meet the diverse needs of young adults.

3. Instruct young adults in the basic information gathering and research skills. These should include the skills necessary to use and evaluate electronic information sources, and to ensure current and future information literacy.

4. Encourage young adults in the use of all types of materials for their personal growth and enjoyment.

5. Design, implement, and evaluate specific programs and activities (both in the library and in the community) for young adults, based on their needs and interests.

6. Involve young adults in planning and implementing services and programs for their age group.

Approved by the Young Adult Library Services Association Board of Directors, June 1981. Revised January 1988. Available at www.ala.org/yalsainfo/competencies.html

Plan for Library Services to Young Adults Hinsdale (Ill.) Public Library

According to the April 11, 1994, *Business Week* cover story entitled "Teens: They're Back," over the next decade the teen population will grow at close to twice the rate of the overall population, transforming our culture and our economy. Here are a few facts to consider:

> One in three teens belongs to a minority compared to one in four of the total population.
>
> One in four households with kids is headed by a single parent.
>
> Teens are "microwave literate," meaning that they are asked to take on more and more adult tasks. For example, 36 percent of teens made themselves meals in 1994, up from 13 percent in 1987.
>
> It was estimated that teens would spend $89 billion in 1995 and that they would influence more than $200 billion in purchases.

The article goes on to describe how advertisers are targeting teens and practicing relationship marketing: "Marketers know that if they attract someone as a teen, there's a good chance they'll keep him or her as a customer in the years ahead." Libraries have a good deal to learn from these advertisers. Those teens will, in many ways, determine how and whether libraries evolve. We need to adapt our services to their wants and needs. They are neither big children nor little adults, but rather a unique population that we cannot afford to ignore.

A 1995 study by the National Center for Education Statistics found that 23 percent of public library users are young adults.* That is, one out of every four individuals who walks through the door of a public library is between the ages of twelve and eighteen (the general guideline for the YA age range). Based on the most current census, children in this age range make up approximately 14 percent of our community's population. Given these statistics, libraries are at a crucial point in making decisions about how we will serve young adults. Teens use libraries for school assignments, advisory services, personal interests, recreational reading, listening or viewing, access to technology, a social gathering place, and sometimes even as a haven from outside pressures. Parents want and expect us to provide quality services for their teenage children as well as their young children. Whether we want them or not, a walk around the library during after-school hours will let you know they are here. Now what are we going to do with them?

What follows is the outline of a plan to serve young adults at our library. As with all library services, staffing, time, resources, and budget have a direct impact on how and when this plan is put into action. It is my hope that the library board, administration, and staff will review the plan, make changes as needed, assign priorities, and develop a timeline for implementation.

I. Young Adult Advisory Board

The development of a Young Adult Advisory Board is the first step toward providing more responsive and effective library and information services for this age group. Meeting with a group of YAs on a regular basis will allow us to discover how teens feel about the library, learn what library services they truly want and need, and help us keep up with constantly changing trends and interests. Through their involvement, YAs will recognize that they can make a positive contribution to their community, learn leadership skills, and develop vested interest in the library.

The Board will be formed by recruiting "regulars" who use the library after school or have participated in past programs. In addition, I will be visiting the schools to distribute surveys on library services and to invite students who are not regular library users to join the board. Once we have a core group, members will help determine how often the board will meet, how it will be organized (formally or informally), and what its initial goals will be. These projects may include ones that

> Survey friends and other teens to find out library needs and interests.
>
> Help create the new YA space by moving, arranging, and decorating the area.

Give suggestions and help plan programs.

Help select books and other library materials.

Produce a library newsletter for teens with book reviews, author interviews, creative writing, program information, and other articles of interest.

Create library displays or bulletin boards.

Put together lists of recommended books on various topics.

Help coordinate special programs.

Provide a YA Board liaison to the library board of trustees.

Raise funds and community awareness.

II. Environment

An inviting and interactive environment that is unique to the needs and interests of young adults is also key to successful YA services. The space should not only contain materials of interest to teens, it should also encourage the use of these materials.

Successful marketers know that location is key to merchandising. The quickest way to lose young adult interest and confidence is to place the YA area near the children's collection. This sends the subtle message that the library considers young adults to be children, while young adults envision themselves as young *adults*. By placing the collection near adult areas they already use, such as magazines, reference, or nonfiction, we send a different message.

Other elements and equipment that are key to creating an environment unique to YAs are:

Clear signage to identify the department, possibly a neon sign.

Decoration: posters from ALA Graphics, movies, and popular magazines.

Comfortable chairs for individual reading.

Tables for study.

Movable shelving for paperback books, display books, books on tape, and videos.

Standard shelving for hardback books.

Shelving for CDs and software.

Slanted shelving for magazines.

Bulletin board or other display space to post local happenings, articles of interest, questions and answers, and so on.

Display space for student art and writing.

Desk for staff.

Access to an online public access catalog (OPAC) terminal and local area network (LAN) terminal.

Suggestion box for programs, good reads, and so on.

III. Collection

Since we are working with limited funding and staff, we cannot expect to meet all the recreational, informational, and educational needs of young adults through the young adult department alone. For the first phase of collection development, our focus should be on creating a popular materials center. Materials to support homework and other educational needs should still be housed in the children's and adult collections.

We should anticipate purchasing multiple copies of popular fiction and nonfiction titles and set up a standing order program for popular series titles. In order to develop a popular materials center that will truly be of interest to YAs, the following collections need to be developed:

Fiction in both hardback and paperback and in multiple copies.

Nonfiction browsing collection of high interest materials.

Magazines including general interest, music, sports, humor, games, current affairs, creative writing, and so on.

Audio collection that includes popular, high-demand performers in CD format.

Books on tape.

Software for use in the library and at home.

A rotating display of adult materials and children's materials that would be popular with YAs.

Again, we will need to focus on marketing the collection by shelving books and other materials face out, by labeling materials by genre, and by creating new and unusual displays that grab the attention of the borrower.

IV. Staffing

Our main concern will be staffing the area to provide reader advisory and ILL/reserve services. Most importantly, we will want to develop a relationship with the YAs so that we can have a better understanding of the services and materials they really need and want. This positive interaction will make the library a more welcoming environment for teens and will help make them continual and responsible library users. Ideally, there would be someone stationed on the YA desk during the busy after school hours and on weekends. During the summer, we would assign a staff member for the morning hours and have teen volunteers staff the reading program during the afternoons. At other times the area would function as a self-service browsing collection. Book displays, bulletin board displays, bibliographies, posted teen reading suggestions, and a comment box should help connect the teens to the collection and services and provide for an interactive environment.

Once we begin to offer special services for YAs, we can count on increased demand for materials, programs, and staff. The library should make it a priority to hire a young adult specialist to fully develop a YA department. At that point, we can make some decisions about adding a formal education support area, creating a homework reserve shelf, and staffing the YA area.

Young adults can be a challenging population with which to work, and staff in all departments will need to be prepared for increasing YA use of the library and its services. Through in-service training we will need to make staff aware of policies regarding access and rights of users of all ages, positive ways to work with young adults, and specific services available for this age group.

V. Programming

The primary focus of programming for young adults is to help them make a connection not only with the library but with the world around them. More than providing entertainment, library programs help YAs get through the process of being a YA:

> Group programs support YAs in their quest for identity and help them feel that they belong.

Programs provide structure in which YAs can socialize and work together.

Informational programs can help answer their questions on topics that range from drug abuse to comic book collecting to getting ready for high school to genealogy.

Programs give YAs a chance to participate in library decision making and to assume responsibilities.

Given the restraints on funding and staff and the time constraints of YAs themselves, programming for YAs will mostly be offered during the summer months and on school holidays. During the summer, a YA reading program and teen volunteers will be the framework around which we plan other special programs. Additional types of programming will include

Educational programs designed to further a YA's general education, either independently or related to school curriculum (SAT workshop, science workshops, Internet workshops, library tours).

Cultural programs that allow YAs to pursue artistic or intellectual pursuits (creative writing, journaling, art shows, book discussions, author visits, and so on).

Informational programs that speak directly to YAs' need to obtain important information about matters that concern them (social, health, or economic issues).

Recreational programs during which they might learn something, but whose goal is to teach YAs that fun and libraries are not at opposite ends of a spectrum (gaming tournaments, crafts, comic book collecting, murder mysteries).

As with programming for children, the library budget will only be able to cover part of the programs we plan to offer YAs. Working with the administration and the board, we will need to explore alternative means of funding such as charging for costs of popular programs, support from the Friends of the Library, sponsorship from community businesses and agencies, and a special "Summer Reading Card" for families from surrounding unincorporated areas. We could also look to other community agencies such as the parks and recreational department, the center for the arts, the community center and youth groups as potential partners for programming.

VI. Outreach

More than with any other population we serve, outreach is essential to connecting YAs and the people who work with them to library services. Communication with the schools is essential. We need to develop a schedule to present a series of booktalks at the middle and high schools and class visits to the library. The youth services department and the reference department can work collaboratively to develop this program. We will also make an effort to keep the schools informed of additional services including assignment alerts, classroom loans, and reading lists. Once a week, we will call the school media specialists to clarify assignments and to find out about upcoming projects.

We will also continue to develop strong relationships with many of the community agencies that work with teens. One idea includes developing a "teen page" in the local newspaper to share information about teen issues and problems. Library staff need to continue to be visible in the community so that parents, teachers, and people who work with youth know more about who we are and what types of service we provide.

Most importantly, we need to make direct connections with the kids. This not only involves talking with YAs who use the library but also getting out into the community and reaching those kids who might not have any idea what the library has to offer. We must go where the teens hang out—Einstein Bagel, the Gap, cafes, music stores, the mall, movie theaters, the pool—to provide program and service information. It would be well worth our time to develop small book displays that we can leave in these locations along with reading lists and copies of the teen library newsletter.

VII. Technology

Computers, CD-ROMs, and the Internet have become standard operating equipment for Young Adults and have a great impact on how YAs search for and process information. As we revise and implement our technology plan, we must remember the needs and interest of our Young Adult users. This may involve providing the following:

An online public access catalog (OPAC) with printer for public use located in the YA department.

LAN terminal with printer for public use.

Personal computers (PCs) and **CD-ROM** collection for recreational and educational use.

Internet access.

Conclusion

Quality library and information service for all is a universal goal of libraries. Limited resources and mandated accountability force library administrators to set priorities and make choices. Because young people are not often advocates on their own behalf, nor are they yet voters, their needs may be overlooked in favor of client groups who are more vocal and who have more power.

---

*U.S. Department of Education, Office of Educational Research and Improvement, National Center for Education Statistics, *Services and Resources for Children and Young Adults in Public Libraries* (Washington, D.C.: U.S. Government Printing Office, 1995).

SOURCE: Adapted from Jane R. Byczek, "Plan for Library Services to Young Adults," Hinsdale (Ill.) Public Library, February 20, 1997.

Basic Rules of Online Safety for Teens

Keep your identity private.

Never get together with someone you "meet" online.

Never respond to e-mail, chat comments, or newsgroup messages that are hostile, belligerent, inappropriate, or that in any way make you feel uncomfortable.

Talk with your parents about their expectations and ground rules for going online.

Check out "Teen Safety on the Information Highway" at www.safeteens.com for more information.

From *Teen Safety on the Information Highway* by Lawrence J. Magid (http://www.safeteens.com). Reprinted with permission of the National Center for Missing and Exploited Children (NCMEC). Copyright © NCMEC 1998. All rights reserved.

Guidelines for Assessing Accuracy and Authenticity in Nonfiction Books

1. Be clear about your definitions of nonfiction, accuracy, and authenticity.

2. Evaluate the experience, training, and track record of the author(s).

3. Evaluate the reputation and track record of the publisher, including whether or not the publisher uses experienced editors, fact checkers, and expert readers.

4. Evaluate presentations of diversity and avoidance of stereotypes in terms of comprehensiveness and integration into the book.

5. Evaluate citations of sources in the footnotes, bibliography, author's notes, and the acknowledgments.

6. Evaluate whether and how source material is used to support assertions and conclusions.

7. Check facts and descriptions against other sources, including your relevant personal experience.

8. Evaluate the visual text for accurate and authentic facts and descriptions.

9. Note reviewers who point out problems with accuracy and authenticity.

10. Scrutinize the book for indications of fictionalizing.

SOURCE: Penny Colman, "Bathtubs, Biographies and Burials: A Guide to Doing Ordinary and Extraordinary Historical Research." Paper presented at PNLA/ILA Joint Conference in Sun Valley, Idaho, August 14, 1998.

Evaluating Young Adult Literature

1. Is the main character between the ages of twelve and eighteen? Most kids prefer to read about characters who are slightly older than they are.

2. Does the book engage the reader's attention within the first few pages?

3. Is the language natural (not too sophisticated or too condescending)?

4. Is the dialogue of the characters similar to the way that real teenagers speak?

5. Does the book avoid lengthy descriptions?

6. Does the book avoid complicated plots or literary devices?

7. Does the book give realistic hope that the problems associated with adolescence can be solved?

8. Is the book interesting and relevant to YA needs and interests?

9. Is the book believable, or does it rely too heavily on coincidence?

10. Are solutions to problems too simple?

11. Is the plot original?

12. Are characters lifelike in responding to situations?

13. Are characters stereotypes?

14. Are characters portrayed in a biased or demeaning way?

15. Is the dialogue natural?

16. Do the characters provide insight into human nature?

17. If the book has a dominant theme, is it imposed forcefully on the plot?

18. Is the tone suitable to the theme?

19. Is the theme suitable for a YA audience?

20. Is the book readable?

21. Is the story imaginative?

22. Is the plot well paced?

23. Is the language suitable to the age and reading level of YAs?

24. Is there a smooth integration of background or factual material?

25. Are there smooth transitions?

26. Is the setting believable?

27. If the setting is real, is it correctly described?

28. If the setting is imaginary, is it consistent throughout the book?

29. Is there enough detail?

30. Is there too much detail?

SOURCE: Adapted from author's notes taken in class of Jane Greene, Media for Adolescents, Catholic University of America, Washington D.C., January 21, 1993.

How to Evaluate Web Sites

The creators of Teen Hoopla (www.ala.org/teenhoopla) offer the following guidelines for selecting Web sites for YAs:

The content encourages exploration and thinking and is appealing and useful to young adults ages twelve to eighteen.

The site is of acceptable quality given its authorship, content, and purpose:

> The source for the content of the site is listed. Author contact information is provided. The source is reputable.

> The information on the site is current. A creation or revision date is provided. Update information is available.

> The site is easy to use and does not require the highest level of technology in order to access its resources.

> The site is free from heavy marketing or promotions related to products sold by the creators or hosts of the site.

If the site is produced by a library:

> The site provides content or information of interest to young adults outside or beyond the host library's community. For example, links to other sites, interactive components, or informational resources not available elsewhere.

> Young adults are involved in some aspect of the creation or maintenance of the site. For example, young adults might select the linked sites, develop content, or create the Web pages.

> ALA's parents' page also lists the selection criteria for the 700+ Great Sites at www.ala.org/parentspage/greatsites/criteria.html

---

SOURCE: Linda Braun, e-mail correspondence, October 5, 1998.

How to Write a Reader's Annotation

A reader's annotation is written to lure someone to want to read a book. It stimulates interest but never gives away the conclusion of a book. It may hint at disaster or triumph but never tells the potential reader what the disaster or triumph is, or how it comes about.

Annotation writing is an art, but it is also a skill that can be acquired with just a little effort. The following questions are a framework to begin with. After a while, these become automatic and a part of a good annotator, just as every other skill acquired ceases to require concentrated thought to be practiced.

1. Who is the central character?

Who is the central character of the work? In most cases, there is only one character to be identified, but occasionally focus on a relative, love interest, the alien, or a foil of the protagonist, depending upon the audience you wish to reach with the annotation.

A central character can be an animal or, on occasion, a machine. No matter. Once you have selected the character, list the character's identifying characteristics. Is she or he an executive, a military officer, an ambassador, a widower, an athlete? How old is the character? Is race or ethnic background an important characteristic?

2. Who are the significant others?

With whom does the central character interact? Nature can be the significant other in a survival story or is it a foster parent, an eccentric hermit, a would-be lover? A dog or horse or cat? You can identify the significant other by the amount of emotional involvement with the central character.

3. *What is the setting?*

Does the action take place in an urban ghetto, a posh suburb, a rural outpost? Are we on a dark and foreboding moor? In outer space? In school?

4. *When does the story take place?*

Are we dealing with the here-and-now, the past, or some future world?

5. *What is the character's challenge?*

Is the character trying to find a place to belong, win a big race, come to grips with sexuality, save humankind from disaster?

SOURCE: Mary Kay Chelton, "How to Write a Reader's Annotation" (A handout from Serving the Underserved II, a seminar conducted by the Young Adult Library Services Association of the American Library Association, January 1996, in San Antonio, Texas), 2-112. Adapted from Dorothy M. Broderick's instructions to *Voice of Youth Advocates* (VOYA) reviewers by Mary K. Chelton, 1996.

How to Write Your Own Booktalk

1. Read carefully, noting any aspects of the book that stand out, such as characterization, exciting scenes, or unique perspectives.

2. Find a "hook." Use the interesting characteristics of the book to entice the reader: describe an interesting character, summarize an exciting scene, or highlight unique perspectives.

3. Write your booktalk as soon as possible after reading the book.

4. Refer to characters and locations by name.

5. In general, try not to exceed one double-spaced page when writing a booktalk.

6. Mention the title and author of the book at the beginning and the end of your booktalk.

7. Write your booktalks in a style that is comfortable.

8. Keep your audience in mind when writing and presenting your booktalks.

9. Be careful not to use stereotypes or generalizations.

10. Don't gloss over significant aspects of a book.

11. Talk to other people about the book, or refer to one of the books on booktalking if you get stuck.

12. Don't give away the ending! Use cliffhangers and interesting descriptions, bearing in mind that your purpose is to encourage the students to read the book themselves.

Tips on Booktalking to a Group

1. Only booktalk books you have read all the way through.

2. Only booktalk books you like.

3. Only booktalk books that you don't mind kids talking about.

4. Practice in front of a mirror or a guinea-pig audience (spouse, children, and so on) before booktalking in front of your real audience.

5. Bring the books with you when you booktalk. Display them in view of the audience. It's great if kids can take the books home with them immediately after the booktalk. If not, consider providing them with a list of the titles you booktalked. This will also help you keep track of what you've done with whom.

6. Bring a copy of your written booktalk with you in case you "space."

7. Don't booktalk to more than one class at a time.

8. Try to choose books with themes that will appeal to your intended audience.

9. Bring books that represent different subjects, genres, and reading levels, both fiction and nonfiction.

10. Choose books with characters who represent different social classes, genders, and racial, ethnic, and religious backgrounds.

11. Allow kids to choose which books they want to hear about first.

12. Pay attention to audience responses and revise your booktalks accordingly.

13. "Cheat" if necessary by marking the backs of books with Post-its to remind you of the names of characters, places, and so on. Also mark passages you intend to read.

14. Consider using booktalks to present curricular themes, new titles, shelf-sitters, and so on.

15. Invite other teachers, librarians, and media specialists to booktalk with you for variety in tone, perspective, and choice of books.

16. Encourage kids to booktalk to each other (and to you)!

School Services Brochure

SCHOOL SERVICES

At the Hinsdale Public Library

Help for teachers and their students in Hinsdale schools.

LIBRARY HOURS

Monday to
Thursday   9:00 a.m. to 9:00 p.m.

Friday   9:00 a.m. to 6:00 p.m.

Saturday   9:00 a.m. to 5:00 p.m.

Sunday   12:30 p.m. to 5:00 p.m.
(From September to mid-June)

Hinsdale Public Library
20 East Maple St.
Hinsdale, IL 60521
986-1976   Fax: 986-9720

1997-98
Jack Hurwitz, Library Director

THE YOUTH SERVICES DEPARTMENT

provides services and materials for toddlers through eighth-graders, their parents, teachers and others who work with young people. School-library cooperation is an important goal; it can benefit all Hinsdale students. The following services are offered to achieve our mutual goal; the education and enrichment of our youth.

THE YOUTH SERVICES STAFF

Jane Bocek, Head of Youth &
    Young Adult Services
Barbara DeLonzio, Assistant Dept. Head
Sue Pajor, Early Childhood Specialist
    Ruth Fasse
    Susan Hatch
    Judy Iyo
    Pamela Mellin
    Sally Monkus
    Deborah Smith

TEACHER LIBRARY CARDS

Teachers employed in any school located within the boundaries of School District 181 are entitled to Hinsdale Public Library Teacher Cards. If you are a new teacher or never had a Teacher Card, you can apply for one in person at the Circulation Desk. If necessary, you can arrange for special classroom loans for particular projects by contacting the Youth Services Department.

TOURS FOR CLASSES AND SCHOOL VISITS

Classes are welcome to visit the library for an orientation and tour. If you would like to schedule a tour of the library for your class, club or other group, please call to arrange a date and time. Instruction in public library use, book talks, story times, tours of library departments and assistance with school projects are some of the programs we offer. We are also available to visit your classroom for special programs. Please allow one month notice when calling to arrange a tour or visit.

INTERLIBRARY LOAN

If the library does not own the materials you need, we can borrow them from another library through the Suburban Library System.

DISPLAYS

We encourage Hinsdale schools to use library space to exhibit art work and other special projects. Sign up forms for the Youth Service Department's monthly art exhibit are sent to the school art teachers at the beginning of the school year. Please contact the Youth Services Department if you wish to exhibit other special projects.

REFERENCE SERVICES

-What information is available on the Great Chicago Fire?

-Are there any reviews of the book *The Giver* by Lois Lowry?

The library staff can help you find answers to questions like these and many others. The answers may be found not only in books, but also in magazine articles, CD-Rom products, on-line databases, videos and special files. Both the Youth Services Department and the Adult Department have reference assistance available all hours the library is open.

BOOK LISTS AND PROFESSIONAL TOOLS

Given one month notification, the Youth Services staff will be happy to provide customized book lists for your classroom needs. We can also provide access to resource materials, book selection tools and professional journals.

ASSIGNMENT ALERT FORMS

When you assign work to your students that involves library research, we do our best to assist them in finding the information they need. By returning a copy of our *Assignment Alert* or by making a simple phone call, you will enable us to set aside the needed materials and to guide your students through their search. If you give annual assignments, your suggestions for additional materials to enhance our collection are welcome.

HOMEWORK RESERVE SHELF

When you notify us of an assignment you've made, we will work with the adult department to pull the appropriate materials and set up a reserve shelf for the students' use. Advance notice also enables us to obtain materials from other sources. By restricting these materials to in-library use, they will be available so that all students can complete the assignment.

TOURS FOR TEACHERS

If you would like to know more about the library's resources or would like to get to know the staff, please call to arrange a personal library tour (for you or a group) or stop by to speak to a Youth Services librarian.

Pathfinder

Debate Topic: U.S. Foreign Policy toward Russia

Before you start your library research . . .

1. Think about ways to broaden your search.

Sometimes you won't be able to find a whole book, article, or Web site on your topic. That doesn't mean there's no information available. It just means you may have to look for smaller pieces, like a chapter in a book, a section of an article, or a part of a Web site.

2. Choose the best place to look.

Some types of sources are better to use for certain topics. For example,

If you're looking for . . .	*try using . . .*
current events	SearchBank
	the Web
an overview of your topic	reference books
detailed, in-depth information	books
recent research or new technology	SearchBank
	the Web
a popular topic and the books	SearchBank
are all out	the Web
	reference books

DYNA

> This is the Library's online catalog where you search for books, videos, CDs, etc., owned by the Library.
>
> Remember to use the bibliography created for you by the Multnomah County Library School Corps.
>
> At the main menu you may select the type of search you'd like to conduct.

Subject Headings (#5)

This command brings up a list of subjects with the headings chosen by the Library of Congress. It works best for broad subjects.

Try: *international relations* OR *United States—Foreign economic relations—Russia*

Super Search (#10)

This command looks for words you type in the title AND the subject headings.

Try: *Russia? foreign policy* OR *Russia relations United States* (The ? asks the computer to search for "Russian" and "Russians" also.)

SEARCHBANK

This is the Library's full text periodicals database. Search the "GEN'L REFERENCE CTR GOLD" database.

Subject Search

Try: *International Relations* (Be sure to check out the "See Also... Subdivisions" link under "Periodical References.")

Keyword Search

Try: *Russia foreign policy United States* (Consider other combinations of keywords that describe your topic.)

WWW

Choose a search engine and type in your keywords.

For example:

go to HotBot (http://www.hotbot.com)

make certain you've told it to search for "all the words"

in the search window type *Russia foreign policy United States*

It's a good idea to try more than one search engine.

Other search engines to try:

AltaVista	http://www.altavista.digital.com
Dogpile	http://dogpile.com
Northern Light	http://www.nlsearch.com
Yahoo!	http://www.yahoo.com

SOURCE: Adapted from Vailey Oehlke, "Barlow High School Debate Topic," Multnomah County (Ore.) Library School Corps, March 12, 1998.

Information Literacy Standards for Student Learning

Information Literacy

Standard 1: The student who is information literate accesses information efficiently and effectively.

Standard 2: The student who is information literate evaluates information critically and competently.

Standard 3: The student who is information literate uses information accurately and creatively.

Independent Learning

Standard 4: The student who is an independent learner is information literate and pursues information related to personal interests.

Standard 5: The student who is an independent learner is information literate and appreciates literature and other creative expressions of information.

Standard 6: The student who is an independent learner is information literate and strives for excellence in information seeking and knowledge generation.

Social Responsibility

Standard 7: The student who contributes positively to the learning community and to society is information literate and recognizes the importance of information to a democratic society.

Standard 8: The student who contributes positively to the learning community and society is information literate and practices ethical behavior in regard to information and information technology.

Standard 9: The student who contributes positively to the learning community and to society is information literate and participates effectively in groups to pursue and generate information.

SOURCE: American Association of School Librarians and Association for Educational Communications and Technology, *Information Literacy Standards for Student Learning* (Chicago: American Library Association, 1998), 8-9.

Programming Tips

1. Think about creating teen programs and services *at* the public library rather than creating public library programs *for* teens. There is a subtle but important difference.

2. Avoid using the terms "teen" and "young adult" as much as possible in publicity materials. Use "middle school/junior high" or "high school students" instead.

3. Ask and involve adolescents at every turn. A youth advisory board is fine, but stretch and reach out to others, too. Structure programs and activities to include the help and opinions of the teens participating at the moment.

4. Understand the developmental and social characteristics of the group, then plan and structure programs and expectations accordingly.

5. Ask the kids to sign up. Even if you have unlimited space, registration gives you an advantage in several ways:

   > You can tell how many kids are coming, which is invaluable in determining supplies and room setup.

   > It provides information about the popularity of the program and allows time to adjust publicity.

   > It creates a list of teens interested in programs at the library.

6. Call those registered the night before the program. At this age, life is hectic and organizational skills are just emerging. A good program is worth "telephone time," so budget time to call everyone registered. No one will ever admit that they've overbooked their schedule, so always ask the real question: "Are you still planning to attend?" Even if they can't come, you've made one more personal contact and have time to call someone on the waiting list!

7. Program content and publicity should be presented with a twist: the unexpected will get your audience's attention.

8. Partner with other agencies to offer a taste of what might be available on a larger or more in-depth scale within the community.

9. Create programs that allow teens to make real contributions to the community. Feature the skills and knowledge they already possess.

SOURCE: Adapted from an electronic discussion list posting by Dana Burton, Youth Services, Monroe County (Ind.) Public Library on YA-YAAC, June 3, 1998.

Sample Young Adult Program Evaluation

1. Have you ever attended a program at this library before?

2. What did you think of the content of this program?

3. How do you feel about the way this program was conducted?

4. How did you learn about this program?

5. Do you think you will attend other programs at this library?

6. What types of programs would you be interested in attending?

7. What is the best time for you to attend programs (e.g., after school, nights, weekends, etc.)?

Age: _____ Grade: _____ School: _____

Library Bill of Rights

The American Library Association affirms that all libraries are forums for information and ideas, and that the following basic policies should guide their services.

I. Books and other library resources should be provided for the interest, information, and enlightenment of all people of the community the library serves. Materials should not be excluded because of the origin, background, or views of those contributing to their creation.

II. Libraries should provide materials and information presenting all points of view on current and historical issues. Materials should not be proscribed or removed because of partisan or doctrinal disapproval.

III. Libraries should challenge censorship in the fulfillment of their responsibility to provide information and enlightenment.

IV. Libraries should cooperate with all persons and groups concerned with resisting abridgment of free expression and free access to ideas.

V. A person's right to use a library should not be denied or abridged because of origin, age, background, or views.

VI. Libraries which make exhibit spaces and meeting rooms available to the public they serve should make such facilities available on an equitable basis, regardless of the beliefs or affiliations of individuals or groups requesting their use.

Adopted June 18, 1948; amended by the ALA Council February 2, 1961; June 27, 1967; and January 23, 1980.
Inclusion of "age" reaffirmed January 23, 1996, by the ALA Council.

The Freedom to Read

The freedom to read is essential to our democracy. It is continuously under attack. Private groups and public authorities in various parts of the country are working to remove books from sale, to censor textbooks, to label "controversial" books, to distribute lists of "objectionable" books or authors, and to purge libraries. These actions apparently rise from a view that our national tradition of free expression is no longer valid; that censorship and suppression are needed to avoid the subversion of politics and the corruption of morals. We, as citizens devoted to the use of books and as librarians and publishers responsible for disseminating them, wish to assert the public interest in the preservation of the freedom to read.

We are deeply concerned about these attempts at suppression. Most such attempts rest on a denial of the fundamental premise of democracy: that the ordinary citizen, by exercising critical judgment, will accept the good and reject the bad. The censors, public and private, assume that they should determine what is good and what is bad for their fellow citizens.

We trust Americans to recognize propaganda, and to reject it. We do not believe they need the help of censors to assist them in this task. We do not believe they are prepared to sacrifice their heritage of a free press in order to be "protected" against what others think may be bad for them. We believe they still favor free enterprise in ideas and expression.

We are aware, of course, that books are not alone in being subjected to efforts at suppression. We are aware that these efforts are related to a larger pattern of pressures being brought against education, the press, films, radio and television. The problem is not only one of actual censorship. The shadow of fear cast by these pressures leads, we suspect, to an even larger voluntary curtailment of expression by those who seek to avoid controversy.

Such pressure toward conformity is perhaps natural to a time of uneasy change and pervading fear. Especially when so many of our apprehensions are directed against an ideology, the expression of a dissident idea becomes a thing feared in itself, and we tend to move against it as against a hostile deed, with suppression.

And yet supression is never more dangerous than in such a time of social tension. Freedom has given the United States the elasticity to endure strain. Freedom keeps open the path of novel and creative solutions, and enables change to come by choice. Every silencing of a heresy, every enforcement of an orthodoxy, diminishes the toughness and resilience of our society and leaves it the less able to deal with stress.

Now as always in our history, books are among our greatest instruments of freedom. They are almost the only means for making generally available ideas or manners of expression that can initially command only a small audience. They are the natural medium for the new idea and the untried voice from which come the original contributions to social growth. They are essential to the extended discussion which serious thought requires, and to the accumulation of knowledge and ideas into organized collections.

We believe that free communication is essential to the preservation of a free society and a creative culture. We believe that these pressures towards conformity present the danger of limiting the range and variety of inquiry and expression on which our democracy and our culture depend. We believe that every American community must jealously guard the freedom to publish and to circulate, in order to preserve its own freedom to read. We believe that publishers and librarians have a profound responsibility to give validity to that freedom to read by making it possible for the readers to choose freely from a variety of offerings.

The freedom to read is guaranteed by the Constitution. Those with faith in free people will stand firm on these constitutional guarantees of essential rights and will exercise the responsibilities that accompany these rights.

We therefore affirm these propositions:

1. It is in the public interest for publishers and librarians to make available the widest diversity of views and expressions, including those which are unorthodox or unpopular with the majority.

Creative thought is by definition new, and what is new is different. The bearer of every new thought is a rebel until that idea is refined and tested. Totalitarian systems attempt to maintain themselves in power by the ruthless suppression of any concept which challenges the established orthodoxy. The power of a democratic system to adapt to change is vastly strengthened by the freedom of its citizens to choose widely from among conflicting opinions offered freely to them. To stifle every nonconformist idea at birth would mark the end of the democratic process. Furthermore, only through the constant activity of weighing and selecting can the democratic mind attain the strength demanded by times like these. We need to know not only what we believe but why we believe it.

2. Publishers, librarians and booksellers do not need to endorse every idea or presentation contained in the books they make available. It would conflict with the public interest for them to establish their own political, moral, or aesthetic views as a standard for determining what books should be published or circulated.

Publishers and librarians serve the educational process by helping to make available knowledge and ideas required for the growth of the mind and the increase of learning. They do not foster education by imposing as mentors the patterns of their own thought. The people should have the freedom to read and consider a broader range of ideas than those that may be held by any single librarian or publisher or government or church. It is wrong that what one can read should be confined to what another thinks proper.

3. It is contrary to public interest for publishers or librarians to determine the acceptability of a book on the basis of the personal history or political affiliations of the author.

A book should be judged as a book. No art or literature can flourish if it is measured by the political views or private lives of its creators. No society of free people can flourish which draws up lists of writers to whom it will not listen, whatever they may have to say.

4. There is no place in our society for efforts to coerce the taste of others, to confine adults to the reading matter deemed suitable for adolescents, or to inhibit the efforts of writers to achieve artistic expression.

To some, much of modern literature is shocking. But is not much of life itself shocking? We cut off literature at the source if we prevent writers from dealing with the stuff of life. Parents and teachers have a responsibility to prepare the young to meet the diversity of experiences in life to which they will be exposed, as they have a responsibility to help them learn to think critically for themselves. These are affirmative responsibilities, not to be discharged simply by preventing them from reading works for which they are not yet prepared. In these matters taste differs, and taste cannot be legislated; nor can machinery be devised which will suit the demands of one group without limiting the freedom of others.

5. It is not in the public interest to force a reader to accept with any book the prejudgment of a label characterizing the book or author as subversive or dangerous.

The idea of labeling presupposes the existence of individuals or groups with wisdom to determine by authority what is good or bad for the citizen. It presupposes that individuals must be directed in making up their minds about the ideas they examine. But Americans do not need others to do their thinking for them.

6. It is the responsibility of publishers and librarians, as guardians of the people's freedom to read, to contest encroachments upon that freedom by individuals or groups seeking to impose their own standards or tastes upon the community at large.

It is inevitable in the give and take of the democratic process that the political, the moral, or the aesthetic concepts of an individual or group will occasionally collide with those of another individual or group. In a free society individuals are free to determine for themselves what they wish to read, and each group is free to determine what it will recommend to its freely associated members. But no group has the right to take the law into its own hands, and to impose its own concept of politics or morality upon other members of a democratic society. Freedom is no freedom if it is accorded only to the accepted and the inoffensive.

7. It is the responsibility of publishers and librarians to give full meaning to the freedom to read by providing books that enrich the quality and diversity of thought and expression. By the exercise of this affirmative responsibility, they can demonstrate that the answer to a bad book is a good one, the answer to a bad idea is a good one.

The freedom to read is of little consequence when expended on the trivial; it is frustrated when the reader cannot obtain matter fit for that reader's purpose. What is needed is not only the absence of restraint, but the positive provision of opportunity for the people to read the best that has been thought and said. Books are the major channel by which the intellectual inheritance is handed down, and the principal means of its testing and growth. The defense of their freedom and integrity, and the enlargement of their service to society, requires of all publishers and librarians the utmost of their faculties, and deserves of all citizens the fullest of their support.

We state these propositions neither lightly nor as easy generalizations. We here stake out a lofty claim for the value of books. We do so because we believe that they are good, possessed of enormous variety and usefulness, worthy of cherishing and keeping free. We realize that the application of these propositions may mean the dissemination of ideas and manners of expression that are repugnant to many persons. We do not state these propositions in the comfortable belief that what people read is unimportant. We believe rather that what people read is deeply important; that ideas can be dangerous; but that the suppression of ideas is fatal to a democratic society. Freedom itself is a dangerous way of life, but it is ours.

This statement was originally issued in May of 1953 by the Westchester Conference of the American Library Association and the American Book Publishers Council, which in 1970 consolidated with the American Educational Publishers Institute to become the Association of American Publishers.

Adopted June 25, 1953; revised January 28, 1972, January 16, 1991, by the ALA Council and the AAP Freedom to Read Committee.

Strategies for Dealing
with Troublesome Behavior

1. *Be consistent.*

   Set standards. Let YAs know your behavioral expectations.

   Involve YAs in decision making concerning behavior policies.

   Respect the rights and opinions of YAs and treat them equally.

2. *Be prepared.*

   When disruptive behavior occurs, you must be prepared to deal with it calmly and quickly.

   Have in place logical consequences that YAs will receive should they choose to disregard the rules.

   Know what problems need immediate attention.

3. *Be firm but fair.*

   Make sure consequences are the same for everyone, regardless of age.

4. *Discipline with dignity.*

   Focus on the inappropriate behavior, not on the young adult.

   Handle individual behavior problems with private conferences when possible. An audience encourages misbehavior.

   Remember how you wanted to be treated when you were a teenager.

   Remember that everyone behaves badly on occasion.

5. *Provide choices.*

   If YAs are to be successful in the real world, they must be capable of making independent, responsible choices.

   When you give YAs a choice, you place the responsibility where it belongs—on the YA.

When you give YAs choices, they learn that they can be in control of what happens to them.

Example #1: "You have a choice. You can either settle down and work quietly or you can leave the library and find somewhere else to work today."

Example #2: "If you choose to continue talking loudly, you will choose to be separated from your friends or to leave the library today."

If YAs don't behave, it's because they've chosen not to or don't know how to.

6. *Be creative.*

The discipline approaches of the past do not work with the YAs of the 1990s.

If one tactic doesn't work, try another one.

7. *Reward positive behavior.*

Give praise or special privileges (popcorn or a snack, lunch with a librarian, computer time, stickers/stamps, YA of the week).

8. *Allow YAs to learn from their mistakes.*

Impress on YAs that future actions will speak louder than words of apology.

9. *Don't label YAs.*

Acknowledge individual differences.

Show genuine interest in YAs.

Give YAs a feeling of community. YAs must realize that they are members of a group and have a responsibility toward that group. If they are to enjoy its privileges, they must accept its duties and obligations.

10. *Know your field.*

YAs will respect you if you demonstrate ability in your field.

11. *Be patient.*

Most YAs can be reached with patience and understanding.

12. *Use your voice and facial expressions wisely.*

13. *Keep a sense of humor.*

Smile.

Lighten up.

A good laugh can save a situation.

14. *Involve law enforcement if anyone's safety is threatened.*

15. *Recognize that YAs are growing up, not grown up.*
    Administer discipline that helps them grow.

SOURCES: Lee Canter, *Lee Canter's Assertive Discipline* (Santa Monica, Calif.: Lee Canter and Associates, 1992).

Richard L. Curwin, *Discipline with Dignity* (Alexandria, Va.: Association for Supervision and Curriculum Development, 1988).

Judy Druse, "Strategies for Dealing with Troublesome Behavior" (from the manual for Serving the Underserved II, a seminar conducted by the Young Adult Library Services Association of the American Library Association, January 1996, in San Antonio, Texas), 3-21.

INDEX

Renée Vaillancourt is the Assistant Director of the Missoula (Montana) Public Library. She received her M.S.L.S. at the Catholic University of America, where she was awarded a U.S. Department of Education scholarship for young adult services. A YALSA member since 1992, Vaillancourt has served on the Quick Picks for Reluctant Young Adult Readers and Youth Participation committees. She has published articles on young adult services in *VOYA* and *School Library Journal* and presented numerous programs and workshops as a YALSA Serving the Underserved trainer.

Mary K. Chelton and **James M. Rosinia** co-authored the predecessor to *Bare Bones Young Adult Services*. Entitled *Bare Bones: Young Adult Services Tips for Public Library Generalists*, it was published jointly by the Public Library Association and the Young Adult Library sServices Association in 1993. Mary K. Chelton is an associate professor in the Graduate School of Library and Information Studies at Queens College. James M. Rosinia has worked as a young adult librarian at the Waukegan (Ill.) Public Library, and as Director of Information Services for the Center for Early Adolescence in Chapel Hill, North Carolina.

Printed in the United States
43859LVS00003B